SHAKY GROUND

WHAT TO DO AFTER THE
BOTTOM
DROPS
OUT

TRACI RHOADES
AUTHOR OF *NOT ALL WHO WANDER (SPIRITUALLY) ARE LOST*

Morehouse Publishing
NEW YORK

Morehouse Publishing, 19 East 34th Street, New York, NY 10016
Morehouse Publishing is an imprint of Church Publishing Incorporated.

Cover design by Dylan Marcus McConnell, Tiny Little Hammers
Typeset by Rose Design

Library of Congress Cataloging-in-Publication Data

Names: Rhoades, Traci, author.
Title: Shaky ground : what to do after the bottom drops out / Traci Rhoades.
Description: New York, NY : Morehouse Publishing, [2022]
Identifiers: LCCN 2022003100 (print) | LCCN 2022003101 (ebook) | ISBN 9781640655591 (paperback) | ISBN 9781640655607 (epub)
Subjects: LCSH: Christian life. | Consolation.
Classification: LCC BV4501.3 .R475 2022 (print) | LCC BV4501.3 (ebook) | DDC 248.4--dc23/eng/20220325
LC record available at https://lccn.loc.gov/2022003100
LC ebook record available at https://lccn.loc.gov/2022003101

*To the communion of saints
(especially those on Twitter),
peace be with you.*

Contents

Foreword

have one pet peeve: *things falling down*. I'm serious. Let a pencil roll off the table, or a book I'm carrying flip to the floor, and I genuinely feel that the universe has affronted me. Personally. Purposefully. *Affronted.*

These are merely inanimate objects slipping out of my grasp; imagine how I feel when *I'm* the one slipping and sliding? A patch of ice on the sidewalk absolutely does me in. The rest of my family walks boldly on, but I hang back, gently picking my way along. Ice skating, skiing, snowboarding—not for me. Growing up in the 1980s, I did spend plenty of happy hours at the roller-skating rink with my friends, but never, ever, did I leave the safety of that oval-shaped carpeted wall. I need something solid I can count on.

Both physically and spiritually I prefer life to be secure, to feel my feet touching the ground, leaving nothing to chance. I want a path that will unfold just as I expect it to. Nothing falling, please. *Certainly* not me.

To my ongoing dismay, life is nothing like this.

In reality, pencils roll, ice is slippery—and that's just the beginning. We're thrown curveballs every day, the unexpected always rising up to meet us. We're on shaky ground in this life. But there are walls around us we can cling to if we know how to find them.

I first met Traci Rhoades on Twitter, and what struck me most about her was her curiosity. Time and again she opened her corner of the internet to questions about faith, life, and community, meandering through our many responses, never becoming lost in it all but never afraid of the chaos either. As I've gotten to know her better—as a writer, a reader, a follower of Jesus, and as a friend— I've discovered that Traci's questions come not from a place of disorientation but from solid ground. She knows who she is and where she stands. That's *why* she's comfortably eager to see what life looks like from where *you* stand too.

This freedom comes through in *Shaky Ground: What to Do After the Bottom Drops Out*, for Traci isn't afraid to be honest about the ways life is unstable, the countless ways the rug is (and will be) pulled out from under us. But as she has wandered and explored, she's found treasures, resources that help hold us up and point our faces forward.

Shaky Ground is a book about Christian spiritual practices, but you almost don't realize it right away. Instead of lecturing the reader with research and how-tos, Traci tells stories—grounded stories, embodied stories. Stories about walking away from a beloved home for the last time, then courageously pointing her feet on the road to a new home. Of gathering with friends to mourn the death of a loved one. Of sitting in a breathtaking cathedral and contemplating the mysteries of faith. And in the midst of all this real-life living, she weaves in the practices of the Christian faith, the walls that hold us up when the ground begins to shake.

Traci writes of the day she walked through a prayer labyrinth, each step leading slowly but surely toward the center. Walking a labyrinth is one of my own favorite ways to pray, and no surprise—following the steadily unfolding path is the very opposite of slip-sliding on ice. But as I read these chapters, the image of a prayer labyrinth stayed with me, for Traci's words have a similar impact as these sacred walks do. She'll lead you with a steady and centering voice, trustworthy and grounded, always beckoning you to take another step yet never leaving you feeling lost or anxious. Slowly but surely, each page will bring you closer to the center.

Are you ready to step inside?

Catherine McNiel
author of *Long Days of Small Things*, *All Shall Be Well*, and *Fearing Bravely: Risking Love for Our Neighbors, Strangers, and Enemies*

THE BOTTOM DROPS OUT

As a little girl, I regularly visited Kansas City's large amusement park, Worlds of Fun. Often, my brothers went with me. My older brother in particular could be very persuasive: as I remember it, he'd always talk me into riding a certain ride with him.

The Finnish Fling.

Now, Worlds of Fun rides take you around the world, which means this ride could be found in the European section of the amusement park. I'm pretty sure a ride like this exists by a variety of names in other places as well. Participants enter a circular barrel and take their spot along the wall. When the ride begins, it spins faster and faster, until gradually the floor drops out, leaving you hanging by centrifugal force. Literally, you stick like Velcro to the wall.

Without fail, this ride left me woozy, sometimes actually making me sick. For at least a few hours, if not for the rest of the day, I felt shaky, and it generally took a while for me to feel settled again.

This book is about that feeling. We're on this ride called life, and we keep expecting it to be *worlds of fun*. But sometimes the bottom drops out, whether by our own doing or not, and we're left wondering how we got here and when this part of the ride will end.

The Finnish Fling shook me up. If I had ignored how I felt and tried to push through, maybe getting a slice of pizza and a slushy, it would not have gone well. This world too offers us quick fixes that might make us feel better for a time. What we need, though, is firm footing. This book is your invitation to look at spiritual practices, some ancient, some new, some seemingly unconventional, that help us live life on solid ground. Ready?

How Do We Follow Jesus?

Everything has a beginning. The teacher in Ecclesiastes alludes to this ("For everything there is a season, and a time for every matter under heaven" [Ecclesiastes 3:1]). I like beginnings. I'm a glass-half-full kind of person and in most cases, the beginning of things is crisp and new. God said it best in the beginning of all beginnings, creation. It was good, good, and very good.

If you are a person of faith—or a person who considers themselves to have once had faith—think back on those beginning days of faith. This book focuses largely on Christianity, those individuals who have placed their faith in the incarnation of Christ, his earthly ministry, death by crucifixion, resurrection three days later, and ascension into heaven. Certainly, there are lessons for others in these pages too. I wanted to be clear about the angle we're taking.

As a Christian, think back on the person, or persons, who introduced you to Jesus, the stories about your baptism or the actual day if you remember it, your first communion, the first Bible you received, the first time you went to church without your parents. If you're not sure you've had these kinds of beginnings, that's okay too. You may discover that you want to find a trusted friend who can talk these things over with you. Maybe today is your own new beginning.

Beginnings overflow with hope. Give a thing enough time, though, and the beginning wears off. It stops feeling new. Things might even start to get shaky. Starting at the beginning of our Bible, we read about the creation of everything. This blissful beginning lasts only two chapters, before chapter three, to which my Bible gives the subtitle, "The First Sin and Its Punishment." Reading on from Genesis, we find a bunch of wandering Israelites in the wilderness, who forgot about their journey to a new beginning, and instead complained about missing the fine food and multiple pairs of sandals they had in Egypt where they were slaves. The world will offer its share of quick fixes, but what we really need is deep, transforming work, and if it takes forty years, so be it. Going on in the Old Testament, it becomes painfully clear that as humans, we need redemption, to be saved from ourselves and the sin that comes between us and our creator.

Turning to the New Testament, we're introduced to our Redeemer, Jesus. In him, we become a new creation (2 Corinthians 5:17). From there, we learn about the beginning of the church. Consider the fifteenth chapter of the book of Acts. A short time before, in the second chapter of Acts, the day of Pentecost was exhilarating. Anything seemed possible with the Holy Spirit to help. Then real people from a wide variety of backgrounds, living thousands of miles apart, had to form the Church. Things got shaken up. A council was convened because the early Christians wanted to know if they should require Gentiles to be circumcised or not. How free exactly was the free gift of salvation? Finally, in books like Revelation, we see that God's plan all along was to restore things. We will someday have a new beginning: "Then I saw a new heaven and a new earth; for the first heaven and the first earth had passed away, and the sea was no more" (Revelation 21:1).

I was baptized at seven years old, and those early days with Jesus went smoothly. I learned the basic Bible stories, memorized verses and hymns, and found that Jesus comforted me every time I came to him with my life circumstances. What a friend we have in Jesus, we'd sing, and it's true. It was only as I became acquainted with people in all their complexity that I began to realize I had put limits on Jesus. As I read my Bible more thoroughly, from cover to cover, I had questions I'd never thought to ask before.

My first church was a small, rural one. I grew up in a church who loved me well, and the people in that church were a lot alike. It got shaky, however, when there were disagreements, like over who should be our next pastor. As I continue maturing in my faith, it's getting even more complicated as I realize Christians who also proclaim the gospel of Jesus Christ can disagree on how we live out that gospel. Living in this world, I also see the quick fixes dangling before me, telling me I can feel better (for a time): things like overspending, overeating, and outperforming. As I mentioned, it's complicated.

For a lot of years I thought the things I did for God—going to church, reading my Bible, having a daily quiet time—would give me a right faith. I thought I'd eventually have an answer to every situation. Jesus told his followers in this world we'd have trouble, but I thought those troubles would be pretty mild, at least in my case. I would read the psalms and think that I didn't really have enemies like that: "Deliver me from my enemies, O my God; protect me from those who rise up against me. Deliver me from those who work evil; from the bloodthirsty save me" (Psalm 59:1–2).

I'm not at the beginning of my Christian walk anymore. I'm out here somewhere in the middle, and I realize I will not find all the right answers. Instead, I'm learning to long for encounters with Jesus, because he's better than knowing every answer and any quick fix. I want to know the God of scripture. I want to be part of the body of Christ in its fullness, blown away by everything the Holy Spirit does among us. I want to surround myself with godly men and women who long for these same things . . .

But back to beginnings. Beginnings aren't always good. Our world is a shaky one, and the sooner we realize things never go exactly as we planned, the better off we'll be. Relinquishing that illusion of control, realizing it often points to a lack of trust, this is the fertile soil God is looking for—to grow our faith. The beginning of a job search after you lose your job, the first Sunday morning at a new church after making the difficult decision to leave an old one, those first lonely days of a new life after your spouse is gone, the early days of a parenting journey with a disabled infant, the devastating appointment where you receive news of a cancer diagnosis. What these beginnings have in common with the good beginnings, though, remains constant. Hope.

> Blessed be the God and Father of our Lord Jesus Christ! By his great mercy he has given us a new birth into a living hope through the resurrection of Jesus Christ from the dead, and into an inheritance that is imperishable, undefiled, and unfading, kept in heaven for you, who are being protected by the power of God through faith for a salvation ready to be revealed in the last time. (1 Peter 1:3–5)

Our hope is not bound by time or circumstance. It doesn't ebb and flow like the world does, based on today's news. Together, we have been gifted this hope through Christ. Like Nicodemus, who asked Jesus how a person could be born again after they were old and already out of their mother's womb, we must hear the words of Jesus, "You must be born from above" (John 3:7). Beginning, middle, and end, it's Jesus, and a life hidden in him, we inherit as our great hope.

Years ago, I spoke at a conference hosted by my local church. A handful of us gave talks that weekend. Mike shared his faith conversion story, telling those who gathered that when he first became a Christian, he kept wondering what he was supposed to do. His pastor and church friends kept telling him to just follow Jesus.

Now, Mike is an intense individual. Even sitting still, even not talking, he still exudes a lot of energy. As he got to this part of his story, he leaned into the crowd, very close to where I sat near the front row, and his voice rose to a shout. He had our attention. "I know I'm supposed to follow Jesus but HOW?" he shouted. That's the question he felt like nobody could answer sufficiently for him.

If we're honest, a lot of us can relate to this question. You look at the world around us and it's all shaky ground, and all the other voices seem so elevated. Whom to believe? What good can you actually do when there are so many problems? Will it ever get better? How did things get this broken?

In these pages, I want to respond to my friend's question, HOW? How do we follow Jesus? More specifically, how do we follow Jesus even in those moments after the bottom seems to have dropped out?

Here's one fundamental truth I've found in following Jesus: We'll find him together. I've become enamored with the vast and wide body of Christ. His Church. From time to time, I step outside of my local church doors, and I might walk into the nave of a nearby Antiochian Orthodox Church. While on vacation, I might look up the time of a local Catholic Mass and visit there, usually on my own. I've begun using prayer books from other church traditions. I use social media as a search engine, finding Christians who aren't exactly like me.

Through these experiences and countless conversations with other Christians, I'm learning more ways to encounter Jesus. I've felt his presence among his people. I've sensed a smile on his face when collectively we sing about wanting to know him. I've tasted and seen that God is good at a number of communion tables. I had no idea how much my connection with Jesus would deepen when I learned to practice silence. A few years back, I went to Mass, and about fifteen minutes before we got started, there was an older gentleman across the room who fingered a rosary and began praying with it out loud. This would seem odd in my church environment, but in this instance, others began joining him in prayer like it was common practice. I could *almost, almost* see Jesus drawing near to hear the prayers of his faithful children. I've learned entirely new ways to pray. How I read the Bible continues to evolve. Can you sense my excitement in inviting you, my brothers and sisters in Christ, to take this journey with me?

In the lighthearted romantic comedy *While You Were Sleeping*, a girl named Lucy falls in love with a man who rides the Chicago L train each day. She's a token taker, and always says "hi" to this man, dressed in fine suits, heading to his important job. One day, a group of muggers push him off the platform onto the tracks in the path of an oncoming train. After being rescued by Lucy, he

remains unconscious and spends some time in the hospital in a
coma. Things get very mixed up, and the man's family (she learns
his name is Peter) ends up thinking Lucy is his fiancée. She goes
along with it for a time, and in the process, gets to know Peter's
entire and altogether lovable family. Eventually, of course, the truth
comes out. Lucy has some explaining to do, as will Peter eventually.

After coming clean about everything that happened, Lucy
stands before the family and says, "The truth is that I fell in love
with you." The family's patriarch gets a somewhat bewildered look
on his face and says, "You fell in love with me?"

"No," she says. "N-o, yes. All of you. I went from being all alone
to being a fiancée, a daughter, a granddaughter, a sister, and a friend."

That's how I feel about all of Christendom. We have so much to
offer one another when it comes to learning to live well in a shaky
world. The practices you'll find in this book are from a Christian
perspective and they all have one thing in common: they mold us
into disciples of Jesus. When established early and repeated regularly, these practices help us face a shaky world with a bold pre-
paredness, instead of reacting out of fear or denial. Some of these
practices, like silence and prayer, carry universal understanding.
Others belong uniquely to our faith. Some of them might not initially seem like spiritual practices at all. Many times in the past
several years I have learned about a certain practice used by other
Christians and thought, oh, that serves the same purpose as when
this other tradition does this other thing. For example, before
beginning a church service, we participate in activities meant to
still our mind, preparing our hearts for worship. In Orthodox
churches, they venerate icons around the room, maybe lighting
candles as well. A Catholic church will have a basin of holy water
by the door, and when parishioners enter, they dip their fingers
in the water before making the sign of the cross. They then walk
to their seat, bowing at the corner of the pew, making the sign
of the cross again, and kneeling on a kneeler while spending time
in prayer. Other churches play worship music quietly, announc-
ing over a sound system when the service is about to begin. For a

time, my own church encouraged attendees to sit in their car, and "park, pause, and pray" before heading into church. They made outdoor tent signs and printed stickers for people to put on their cars as a reminder.

Our experiences have taught me, and any number of Christians throughout time, how to follow Jesus, to build a foundation when everything around us feels unsteady and unreliable. Through these actions we are ushered into sacred spaces where we meet with a loving God. It's here we realize how much he loves us. It's here that we can lay down our burdens at the foot of the cross. If we follow these practices often enough—a quick search on the internet tells me it takes an average of sixty-six days to form a habit—we actually establish spiritual habits that anchor us in Christ. Abiding in Christ like this, day after day, year after year, that's how we find our footing when things get shaky.

It is as the old hymn "Turn Your Eyes Upon Jesus" instructs us: look to him, the things of earth will go strangely dim (not yet fading altogether), and there it is for us to grasp, the light of his glory and grace.

What do we do after looking full in his wonderful face and seeing the light of his glory of grace, as the song instructs us to do? In the words of Jesus:

You are the light of the world. A city built on a hill cannot be hid. No one after lighting a lamp puts it under the bushel basket, but on the lampstand, and it gives light to all in the house. In the same way, let your light shine before others, so that they may see your good works and give glory to your father in heaven. (Matthew 5:14–16)

We let our light shine.

Friends, we cannot conjure up this light on our own. It's always and forever through Jesus. How do we keep shining in a world that's shaky and unpredictable?

Here's how.

PART I
SOLID GROUND

CHAPTER 1

Things Have Always Been Shaky

My heart has no desire to stay where doubts arise and fears dismay; Though some may dwell where those abound, my prayer, my aim, is higher ground.

—Johnson Oatman Jr., "Higher Ground"

esus of Nazareth walked the earth during a difficult chapter in Jewish history. Let's review with the briefest of overviews. Toward the end of the time in which the events of the Old Testament occurred, the Assyrians took over the Northern Kingdom, sending thousands of Israel's people into exile. The Babylonians, who conquered the Assyrians, took over the Southern Kingdom, sending thousands of Judean people into exile. King Cyrus of Persia, who took over the Babylonians, sent the Judeans home, except they didn't all return. Some of them had grown accustomed to where they were. It can be hard to pick up and move again. In the four hundred years between the events of the Old Testament and New Testament, the Greeks took over the Persians. Then, in 63 BC, the Romans took over the Greeks. The Romans dominated the civilized world, and the Jewish people found themselves overtaxed and living in a land occupied by a foreign army. Revolts were common and there was much political unrest.

This is the world Jesus entered. Perhaps every generation before us has uttered similar words, but those tumultuous times in Jesus's day, they feel an awful lot like our world: corrupt government officials, capital punishment, racial tension. These times too were shaky.

Read a daily newspaper. Turn on the morning news. Check your social media feed. We do live on shaky ground. Maybe today is worse than twenty years ago. A hundred years ago. A thousand years ago. Worse than it was in Jesus's day. Or maybe the world's always been shaky. No doubt current events point to a broken world. Violent shootings, terrorist activity, terminal and chronic illnesses, life-altering global viruses, are not nothing. But maybe we could assuage our anxiety, our deep-seated fears, if we regularly determined we would cling to our Savior. Maybe the lesson we need to internalize deeply is that we live in a fallen world. It is Christ alone who is the same yesterday, today, and forever (Hebrews 13:8).

If it is true, the things that are the dire matters of our day are in fact legitimate causes for concern, but there have always been causes for concern in this world, then what Jesus told the large crowd gathered on a mount in his day is still true for us: "So do not worry about tomorrow, for tomorrow will bring worries of its own. Today's trouble is enough for today" (Matthew 6:34).

I grew up singing the old hymns. We sang the same ones so often, I find I've tucked them away deep in my subconscious. Many times, as I go through the day, lines will bubble up. Friends, if our world is indeed unstable and always has been, there's a hymn, or two, for that.

"On Christ the sold rock I stand; all other ground is sinking sand. All other ground is sinking sand."

"Rock of ages, cleft for me, let me hide myself in thee."

I don't know if it's my age or the times we live in, but I feel as if things have gotten more complicated. What I want to communicate clearly right here at our beginning is that, according to Jesus, "In the world you face persecution" (John 16:33), and "He makes his sun rise on the evil and on the good" (Matthew 5:45).

Nothing in our shaky world surprises God, and it is Christ alone who has overcome the world.

So here we are, in a world that's always been more than a little wobbly. Once we acknowledge this fact, our next question should be, what can we do about it?

A side note: the previous sentence doesn't say what can *I* do about it. For far too long, we've been walking around in a me-first individualistic society (at least in the part of the world I call home) and that might be a big part of the problem. At our roots, we are self-absorbed, while Jesus calls us to root ourselves in him. We are designed to walk through this world together. In Christ, we can better help one another and accept help from others.

Collectively standing firm, even when the ground below goes topsy-turvy, will require something from each of us. For Christians, it means learning to lean on Jesus (there I go with another hymn). The good news is he doesn't expect us to figure this out on our own. He's given us spiritual actions we can take to draw nearer to him. He is there, waiting to be found, and through times of stillness, prayer, taking in scripture, reciting creeds, and other ways we'll explore, the Church can be reminded our one foundation is Jesus Christ our Lord (closing out with a hymn).

CHAPTER 2

Silence as Medicine

Weary or bitter or bewildered as we may be, God is faithful. He lets us wander so we will know what it means to come home.

—Marilynne Robinson, *Home*

t took us three years to sell our house. It took another few years to purchase a piece of property and another year to build a new home. There's a lot more to this story, but for now, I want to focus on how God led me home.

We bought the property where we live now in the springtime. I remember because I used to drive out here when it was still quite cold. The weather takes forever to warm up in Michigan. The dirt roads that took me a few miles off the highway were still frozen, so I didn't get any dust on my car. When you turn onto the road to our then newly purchased property, there's a DEAD END sign. It's not a through road. I remember thinking, that's fine because this road is going to lead to my new home, and I don't need it to go anywhere else.

Bundled up in a coat and hat the first time I saw the property, I remember turning my face into the wind. There was a grassy two-track that led to the hillside overlooking the pond. It felt bitterly cold standing there looking over the land, the hills, the trees, the water. My soul was exhausted: all those times we had a house showing, and potential buyers found reasons not to go through with the purchase; the houses we looked at in what we kept hearing was a "buyers' market" without ever finding the right house for us. We didn't have plans to move again anytime soon, if ever. We were looking for a forever home. Brothers and sisters, aren't we always doing this? Oh, how I longed for it.

Standing on top of a hill, I sensed the presence of God hovering over me, indeed all around me. "You will heal here," God whispered to my spirit. The beauty, the seasons, the time alone, and the solitude—God had brought me here, and I knew I'd emerge whole again.

Healing has layers. I sensed there was an even deeper work God wanted to do in me. Dad had died six years prior to that spring, and after his death, we eventually sold the family farm in Missouri. We moved there when I was three years old. It had been in our extended family for three generations at that point. As a child, I didn't remember living anywhere else. I must have ridden my bike up and down our gravel road what feels like a thousand times. The neighbors mostly stayed the same. There was a creek in the backyard, and when my big brother let me tag along with him and his friends, I inevitably walked too close to the water's edge and fell in. We'd hunt mushrooms and pick blackberries according to the seasons. My dad built a big pole barn, and I can still hear my brother's baseball ricocheting off its metal walls as he played catch for hours. I didn't realize it then, but a place can get inside of you.

Dad passed away suddenly. I'd been married for a few years and hadn't lived at home for some time. Still, I took for granted this particular spot on earth would always be in our family. Growing up, it had been Mom who oversaw the finances. In my mind, I see my parents seated at the dining room table, her trying to get him to focus on paying bills and doing tax paperwork. When my parents divorced, Mom moved into town and Dad stayed on the property, as it originally belonged to his side of the family. I gave little thought to who managed the budget then. In my twenties, I was forging my own way in the world. I had no idea what financial state the home place was in, didn't know Dad had used it as collateral to get himself out of other debts. Reader, I need you to know drugs and alcohol play a role in this story. I didn't know the price these vices would demand of my family. More than we could afford. Good Christian girls aren't supposed to know such things. We planned Dad's funeral, buried him in a simple pine box, and spent our initial grieving months, on into years, putting together the financial puzzle he'd left behind. Looking back, I'm thankful we didn't know right away we'd have to sell our land. God, in his providence, revealed this reality piece by piece.

I sat with my mother-in-law on their front porch one afternoon, updating her on Dad's estate. I still remember how surreal it felt to learn new terms like "executor," "probate court," and "estate planning."

"We're going to have to sell everything," I told her, delivering the news in a monotone. I felt all cried out over the saga of the last few years.

"Isn't there anything you can do?" she replied. "It's terrible you can't keep the land in the family."

"This would have been impossible to fathom in the early days of grief. But now, I know we've walked every step of the process, and we've accepted this is the way things have to be."

Acceptance doesn't mean I liked it. Going off to college, living in the city, settling in a new state, I'd never considered there might come a day when home wouldn't be there. When my husband and I built our new house, we, along with our daughter, put our hands in the fresh concrete on the back porch, like I did when we poured the steps on the back porch of my childhood home. Are my handprints and those of my brothers still there, or have they been worn down by the tread of strangers' footprints, erased by the elements of snow, rain, and ice over the years?

I have a deep attachment to open spaces. Two times in my life I have felt like I could call a place home, and both were in a country setting. It's possible this is genetically wired in me. I come from a line of country people, many of them farmers. On both sides of my family, mothers have lost their children. My Grandma Lucy, my mom's mom, lost two teenagers within a year of each other, both to car accidents. Years later, she'd lose another son in a car accident, within a year of losing her husband to complications from Alzheimer's disease. Yet, in all my years of spending time with Grandma

Lucy, she never appeared bitter. When I was growing up, our family didn't talk much about the aunt and uncle I had never met. We did share stories about Uncle Lonnie, but mainly because my generation all remembered him. Now that I'm older I wonder what it must have been like for her. My mom remembers Grandma spending a lot of time in her bedroom when her two teenage children passed away. People would stop by to offer help or bring a casserole dish, and she told Granddad he'd have to take care of things. There is some business that's only between us and God.

Where Grandma lived it was quiet too. A house at the end of a long lane, surrounded by acres of farmland and some livestock. Did the land help her heal? With other children to raise and chores to do in the house and around the farm, she couldn't stay confined for long. There was always something to do. Perhaps putting her hands to work again also helped with her healing. Work keeps our mind from focusing on things we cannot change.

I remember the early days of walking around our new property. My husband mowed paths throughout the acreage, and I spent time learning what seasons delivered which wildflowers, noting what high winds and strong rains do to the mature trees along the trails. I let myself acknowledge this place didn't feel like home yet. Not like the place where I'd grown up in rural Missouri. I was thankful to be in the country again, but had no idea how long it would take for this new place to settle in me. God reminded me to be patient.

In my beginning days on this new piece of land, staring out over these hills, I also acknowledged I had a lot of emotional work to do. Losing a childhood home, being without a home of our own for several years, I'd expressed how I felt about all this to God, to my mom, husband, and a few close friends, but a number of words remained unspoken: words that wouldn't change anything; words that only wore rings around our circumstances. I was bone weary. From thinking back on how my brothers and I lost our dad, but also all the ways we never really had him. From trying to find a home, wondering why it was taking so long, and trying desperately to figure out what God might be trying to teach me so we could hurry up and move on to other life lessons. I thought back on discussions my husband and I had about what our next steps should be, the times we agreed and the times I gave in, swallowing harsh words of frustration. We'd had our daughter while in between homes. Would we be able to give her a sense of home like my husband and I had both known?

Now, here we were. I knew how to do country living. I felt confident the solitude found in this space, the silence that only comes here in the middle of nowhere, would act as a balm to my soul. I could finally give a proper goodbye to my childhood home and replace it with these trees and body of water, alive among this wildlife. No, not that this new place would replace my childhood home, but it could serve as a tender reminder of what it's like to let a place take up residence inside of you.

I was ready to heal. It didn't happen in a few days. There have been ups and downs, steps forward and back again. As God and I spent time together here, he would bring to mind areas where I needed to repent. Sometimes that meant an apology to someone in my life. Other times, I had to forgive myself. In each case, repentance meant ultimately turning to God again. It always means that—it's the ongoing work of one of my favorite church words, sanctification. Being confident that he who began a good work in you will be faithful to complete it (Philippians 1:6). These years here have been good for me and my family. Dad would have liked it here.

We don't all live in the country, of course. That's my story, but there are other versions of our need for place. There are other definitions of home, and what that means in a life. The quiet, the hay fields, the rolling hills, these all help ground me, providing space for healing. I also had to be a willing participant in the process. My mind had to stop overthinking, slow down, and become still. That's what home, both a physical location and a spiritual posture, does for us. If somewhere in the process I had realized I needed professional help to heal, I would have sought out a therapist. I have in the past, and it helped.

In addition to quieting the world around me and in me so that I can experience healing, I've learned to offer my thoughts, my days, up to God. A prayer of Examen is an ancient method developed by Saint Ignatius of Loyola. It looks intently at the entirety of a day's activities and provides the space to interact with it. Start by asking the Holy Spirit to guide your thoughts. Look back over the day and express your thanks for the good things that happened, even on those days when it's tough to find things to name. Examine the feelings that come up as you consider the day. Pray about the activities, the people involved, how it all made you feel. Where are the moments that call for repentance and the need for new direction? Offer those confessions in prayer. When were the times of deep awareness of God's presence, regardless of the circumstances? Offer gratitude. For me, during this time God also regularly brings to mind people who could benefit from my attention in some way. It might be someone who needs prayer, and I might know the specific need or I might not. I have sent notes and texts out of these daily Examen prayers. Sometimes there are people I have offended, or need to be more patient with, or should forgive. The guidance I receive isn't aways easy, but I have come to trust it as helpful and true, from the source who holds all things together.

Looking toward tomorrow, practicing the Examen, ask God to reveal even more of himself to you. This should be a slow process, with moments of silence in between. You don't have to set a timer but make silence a natural part of the prayer. What does God have to say in response to your day? If praying the Examen before bedtime, what do you need to offer up to him in order to get a restful night's sleep? As Aaron Niequist writes in his book *The Eternal Current*, "The Examen is not primarily a self-help technique or self-examination process; it is a way to create holy space in which to carry on a holy conversation."

This kind of prayer is intentional. It incorporates intentional silence because, remember, prayer is a conversation with God. We can't always be interrupting him with our thoughts and words. It's also an intentional invitation to invite God into some moments

with you. An invitation he will never turn down. As I've implemented spiritual practices like the Examen, I have sensed God
is pleased with me. I notice his presence in my daily life more.
In a conversation with my friend Beth, she shared, "I grew up in
church but through counseling I am just now realizing God doesn't
just love me, he likes me. He wants to hang out with me." It's true,
for Beth, for me, and for you. Isn't it something? The God of the
whole universe wants to spend some time with us. He will sustain
us, no matter what comes.

From these days of learning to settle my spirit, I also have taken
to envisioning myself being at home with Jesus. I spend time pic-
turing Jesus, inviting him to do his work in me. In my mind, I see
myself sitting before him, often with hands extended, palms up.
Here, I offer him the disappointments, the unspoken words, all that
remains unknown in my future. My spirit acknowledges receiving
from him everything I need to move forward. Ultimately, he is our
great healer. Our job is to find the place and the internal space for
him to do it.

CHAPTER 3

A Deeper Work

We can cultivate a growing awareness of serving God, of nurturing and creating life. We can practice the presence of God. We can learn to live meditatively.

—Catherine McNiel, *Long Days of Small Things*

When you live out in the country, you don't go somewhere every day. In our household, we make lists of errands to run in town and when we go in for another reason—church, a meeting, or an after-school activity for my daughter—we check those things off the to-do list. We live a distance from our church, too, and this is often hard for me. Sometimes I convince myself the best way to show God I love him is to show him how busy I can be for him. At times, my idea of a righteous faith looks like being at all the committee meetings, attending every church service, and regularly scheduling in-person appointments. I feel as if this somehow makes me important?

In reality, those times I feel most in the center of God's purpose for me, I'm at home surrounded by stillness. I realize this is not the pathway he has for all of us, the amount of solitude I require, but it's how he has fashioned me. I flourish in being alone, where I read the books, spend time praying, take in my Bible, and write. On my best days, I shush the voice trying to tell me if I really loved the people of God, I'd be among them, serving them all the time. Even those more inclined to be a Martha (Luke 10:38–42) cannot sustain ongoing hospitality without stopping to let Jesus fill their own cup.

Sometimes getting quiet, and giving my thoughts a rest, looks like hanging clothes up on the line outside. Walking down my long driveway to get the mail. Sitting on my back porch with a good book. Gathering eggs out of the chicken coop. In these moments outside, I take deeper breaths, I notice the tomatoes are almost ripe for the picking, I watch the butterflies flutter from flower to flower in the tall grass, I smile at my dogs running and rolling in the dirt, and I delight in the birds rushing to the feeders.

We minister to one another out of the experiences of our real life. God and I spend a lot of time together here in the countryside. I'd like to share with you what he's taught me about silence.

Before we begin, I want you to be prepared for what silence might reveal. Chances are, as you develop a rhythm of silence, you'll begin to face hard things: about yourself, about your past, about others. Why would we want to do this? One of the primary reasons is this: in practicing silence as a spiritual discipline, we invite Christ to walk with us as we make these discoveries. Those rare moments when I feel especially close to Christ, close enough to almost reach out and touch him, they are worth any trepidation I might feel. To sit in his presence and bask in the great love he has for me, for all of us, is worth the effort.

Here's an example of a time when a personal struggle of mine broke through the solitude, and God helped me work through it. I had spent a calm, relaxing day at home, relishing the quiet. As I went about my day, God and I had been in conversation. That afternoon, I received a text from my in-laws. They planned on asking our pastor to their house for dinner and if they secured a date and time, would it be possible for us to join them?

This wasn't an unusual request in any way. My father-in-law is an elder at our church. Pastors go to people's houses for dinner on occasion, or at least I think they do. We'd invited this particular pastor to our house a handful of times over the years, and it had yet to work out. I knew it wasn't intentional, but plans hadn't ever come together. Here's the thought that went through my mind immediately after reading the text, "Oh, of course he'll go to their house for dinner. A pastor wouldn't want to have dinner at your house because your dad didn't go to church." Tears sprang to my eyes.

This accusation had nothing to do with the conversation at hand. Interrupting my day of silence, disrupting the peace in my home, was the father of lies. One of my deepest wounds is that my dad didn't go to church. It's fed my feelings of rejection a number of times over the years. This accusation left me furious, and suddenly I realized the target of my fury. This was not a lie I was going to believe anymore. I am not a second-class church citizen because I don't come from a picture-perfect Christian home. God did not think any less of me because my parents' house wasn't one where pastors came to have Sunday dinner. I tell you this story as one example. It might come as a surprise what lies fester deep in your soul. Know this. We carry no shame in Jesus. He wants to restore our dignity, for us to see ourselves how he sees us.

If the silence is difficult for you, and what comes to mind is more than you can handle alone, there are counselors who can help you. There is no one more trustworthy with these deepest parts of yourself than Jesus, but he's willing to partner with others who can help. In this instance, he and I went to work digging this lie up and throwing it on the figurative trash heap.

Looking back over the years I've lived in our home, I'm thankful. This is but one example of God and me weeding out deep-seated lies. I don't have to tell you how noisy our world is—inside and out. One of many ways we distract ourselves from the difficult task of facing that work of weeding is to keep busy, unable or unwilling to quiet ourselves before God. Before we look at any other way to know Jesus more, we have to find silence within. It's where God does his best work. It's where I do important healing work with him in my own life. Imagine if we walked through life as a deeply healed people.

Again, I'm not talking about doing away with therapy, or prescribed medication, because those can be necessary parts of spiritual health as well. I'm talking about men and women who have realized the benefits of communing with God in solitude.

We don't all live in a rural setting, but it's imperative we find a space for stillness, whatever that looks that in our own lives. In his book *The Deeply Formed Life*, pastor Rich Villodas emphasizes the importance of this in his own urban lifestyle:

> We live in the city that never sleeps and have the same struggles of every city dweller. I note this because most books about spiritual formation are often written with mountains, the woods, and monasteries pristinely positioned in the background. I write, think, and live with the background of sirens blaring, homeless men pouring into our church building for showers, and neighbors frantically running to catch the subway. The deeply formed life is not simply for people who have the benefit of environments conducive to silence and solitude. From personal experience, I can assure you that it's for people of all walks of life who long to be shaped by God's gracious love.

The practice of silence may say more about the state of our spirit at any given time than it does about present circumstances. I'm more introspective by nature and have spent most of my life in the country, so silence comes more naturally to me. I'm also a reader, and that has taught me to drown out the world's noise as I get lost in a book. In these ways, silence has become a friend and steadies me. But what about those of you who are more prone to action? You spend a few moments in silence, praying, and then feel the urge to get to work. There's a lot that needs fixing in this world, and you want to do your part to help. Spending time with God in silence offers faithful guidance, so you can home in on those things he's given you the greatest passion for and move forward in a focused way. We should want to do the work God has for us to do, but this needs direction. If we have spent the time needed with God in silence, and gotten our marching orders, so to speak, when the work gets hard, and it will, we don't get discouraged and quit. We're allowing him to continue forming us along the way, doing the good work we do in Jesus's name, trusting him with the outcome.

The world needs both types: those who spend a good amount of time contemplating, and those who are on the go, ready to take action. And we all need silence. Silence creates the space for us to give our true selves to God, so we don't drown in things like bitterness and worry and anger. It gives us time to refocus on those things that matter most in a situation, and to know he is God.

For some of you, silence is a burden you carry. You find yourself alone most days, and the silence begins to feel like a disease, affecting your mind and your spirit. Yes, we need stillness to quiet our mind and let God do his good work, but we aren't meant to be solitary creatures. Allowing for the fact that we're all in different life stages, I'd encourage you to consider the other spiritual practices we'll look at here in this book. Maybe you'll discover some things you can do in a small group or church setting. May we all find a healthy balance between solitude and companionship.

My husband and I have a middle schooler. Prayers appreciated and accepted. I remember how excited she was to start sixth grade. She got her own locker and would have a greater sense of freedom as students would now switch classes throughout the day. One of the first things these students do to kick off their three years of middle school is take a trip to sixth-grade camp. My daughter was so excited to go, but came back a little quiet. It didn't sound like anything major had gone wrong, but things were definitely off. What ensued from there was a year of friendship shifts. Thankfully she talked to us about it, and we had some good conversations about how these years were about young people learning to find their way, discovering who they are, what their social circles will look like, etcetera. Her tears that year nearly broke my heart, and God had to teach me, is still teaching me, I cannot fix all her problems. These ups and downs help her know how to navigate all of life, because those relationship problems don't go away when we move on from middle school. When she became a teenager, still hanging out in middle school, our one-on-one time wasn't always spent talking. I call these non-talking times together a "ministry of silence." We would sit together, maybe eating a snack or driving in the car. We discussed what it looks like to sit with God this way too, praying and asking for guidance in situations. I often feel like I'm teaching my daughter skills I'm learning myself, but I see her taking in the same lessons I have learned: God forms us in these silent times with him. I see her growth and maturity as a young woman of God, and I am thankful.

A popular hymn, *In the Garden*, talks about walking with God:

I come to the garden alone,

While the dew is still on the roses,

And the voice I hear falling on my ear

The Son of God discloses.

It surprised me to learn, when this hymn first came out, it met with some controversy. Lyricist C. Austin Miles said he received the lyrics to this hymn in a vision. This did not sit well with more conservative Christians. Published in 1912, the lyrics were identified as overly intimate, even being excluded from earlier editions of hymnals. I'll be the first to admit I don't fully understand terms like "mysticism" and "spirituality" and "meditation." I've learned, though, if you're going to spend this kind of quality time with Jesus, it's going to get intimate.

I have never heard the audible voice of God. However, I know the affinity Mr. Miles writes about in the hymn. The longer I walk with Jesus, the better I recognize his voice. The more I obey what he asks me to do, the easier it is to trust him with everything in my life. The more I trust him, the more I love him. That is what happens on the gravel road in my neck of the woods, but I've also had it happen in a busy airport, loudspeaker blaring and children bumping into my luggage. It can happen anywhere. As you'll see in the next chapter, our Quaker friends in particular have much to teach us about developing this kind of silence.

CHAPTER 4

Silence in Church

You don't need to unburden or collect yourself and then come to Jesus.

—Dane C. Ortlund, *Gentle and Lowly*

n my expansive approach to Christianity, I often come across the term "liturgy." In its most basic form, liturgy is an order of events used in a time of worship. We worship in unique ways. When I visit other churches, I am often introduced to new forms; some I had not heard of or experienced before. Even things that might seem basic to other Christians—like corporate confession, reciting the creeds, and silence—are unfamiliar to me. I've spent a fair amount of time thinking about each element of liturgy, considering how it might benefit us to do some of the things we typically do alone, in a communal setting. The benefits, it would seem, are many. Our examination of silence would not be complete if we didn't consider how it might benefit us to incorporate moments of silence in corporate worship.

My friend Brent Bill is a Quaker minister. He sent me a private message on Twitter on a day we were talking about silence in the church. Or, in the contemporary worship style of my local church, the lack thereof. Brent asked if he could have his publisher send me a copy of his book *Holy Silence*. I rarely turn down a free book.

Brent's book introduces readers to the Quaker tradition. One of the gifts they've given the wider Church is a better understanding of silence. Toward the end of his book, Brent tells about a place he

and his wife visit—Bald Head Island (BHI)—off the coast of North
Carolina. It can only be reached by ferry, as cars are not allowed on
the island. I frequent Mackinac Island in Michigan, so I've already
got a picturesque scene of BHI in my mind. From what I know of
Quakers, it seems like their kind of place.

Every Sunday, an ecumenical group gathers for worship at Village Chapel on the island, and over the years, Brent and his wife
became involved enough with the group that Brent was invited
to be a guest minister, which means he leads that week's worship
service and is also available in case an emergency pastoral call is
needed. On the weeks Brent leads worship, he introduces the
group to the Quaker idea of holy silence. The congregants have
been receptive to this concept, and it has become something he
offers each time he leads the service. In *Holy Silence* he writes:

> I say that Quaker worship is based in silence because we
> gather in community to hear God's voice. I often say some-
> thing about how busy and noisy our lives are, so one of the
> great things about worship is that we can come together, be
> still, and listen, and that our worship this morning will offer
> opportunities for just that.

As part of this idea that Brent sometimes describes as "waiting
worship," he intentionally inserts holy pauses within the service.

> "If you're following along in your bulletin, and something
> doesn't happen right away, don't worry," I assure them. "It
> doesn't mean that I or the choir have lost our place." There's
> usually a chuckle or two at that.

When I first read about his approach at Village Chapel, a familiar sense of holy envy rose up inside of me. I mentally added Village
Chapel at Bald Head Island to my ever-growing list of churches to
visit. I wondered what it would be like to add pauses like this to a
worship service without it feeling uncomfortable to those of us who

are not acclimated to it. I grew curious about the sense of collective calm these individuals might feel as they sat in silence together.

The church I attend might feel familiar to you. Our praise band consists of keyboards, guitars, drums, and singers. A few times over the years, they have added a harmonica, accordion, or banjo. I'm all about shaking up the routine.

But we don't have silence. When we enter the lobby, music is playing. There's a recorded voice telling us the worship service will start in a few minutes. During times of prayer, the worship leader plays his guitar softly. We start with a song and end with a song. On the third Sunday of each month, when we have communion, there's music playing as we go forward to receive the bread and wine (grape juice). I remember a few times we've had silence, but it was exactly for the reason Brent referenced in his announcement: someone missed their cue. This was not a holy silence. It was the kind of silence a staff member was going to have to answer for on Monday morning.

Occasionally, our church has tested out a few minutes of silence during prayer—okay, maybe more like thirty seconds—to see how it would go. Even in secular settings like a public meeting or a sporting event, we are familiar with the idea of a few moments of respectful silence. It can't be that hard to do during church. For a time, I gave the morning welcome and shared any announcements at our church. In the prayer leading us to the singing portion of the service, I remember calling the congregation to a moment of silent prayer a few times. My heart accelerated a little as I wondered how much silence would be socially acceptable among this crowd who was largely unfamiliar with it. Another time, our worship leader tied moments of silence in with a formal prayer. It was uncomfortable; I could feel it. Still, I was thankful we tried it. I found him after the service and told him I thought it was a good first effort. How can we get used to something if we never give it a first awkward try? We haven't done anything like that since.

Leadership plays a big role in the willingness to try something new in a service. You might be asking, Why do we need to implement silence? What good is this going to do our community? Walking together as a community of believers means we'll go through highs and lows together. In the years I've been at my current church, we've built a new building, sent people on mission trips, hired and said goodbye to various staff members, lost beloved church members, and seen a number of committed families come and go. We're a part of one another's lives and a lot has happened in our time there. A period of silence among a church family gathered together in worship helps us absorb what we're experiencing. It gives the Holy Spirit an opportunity to speak into our collective lives and guide our steps. Things like silence open our hearts to more fully receive what God has for us.

There are times we have to practice silence, or any new thing we try, awkwardly. If silence isn't familiar to you, either in your prayer at home or in worship settings, start small: thirty seconds, with a deliberate explanation about how people might "use" the time. Acknowledge that it's probably going to feel awkward—and that's okay. Work with silence in your community gatherings. What might it feel like to take a collective breath together? Is this a humbling act in any way? See what God might show you.

In my church visits, I can think of several times I've noted moments of silence. It still catches my attention, but I've gotten more accustomed to it with time. In a Methodist church once, they passed the offering plates. After the plates had made their way around the sanctuary, the pastor took the offering, walked into the chancel in silence, and lifted the monetary offering up at the altar. He prayed God would receive the first fruits of the congregation. Another time, my daughter and I visited a Stations of the Cross service at an Episcopal church. Traditionally, the stations of the cross are a series of stops designed for contemplating the various parts of Jesus's walk to Golgotha. Often, the various stations are depicted in pictures hung around the walls of a sanctuary, which is how this church had them displayed. A group of about ten of us went around the room, doing a short reading and prayer at each station. We took turns reading, so there were moments of silence as we waited for the next person to volunteer. Movement from station to station was done in silence as well. Waiting for a reader felt odd the first few times, but once we settled into the silence, it felt appropriate. In a way this process brought our group together, as we individually reflected on the path Jesus took, but did it in community.

I've noted a number of silent moments during Catholic Mass: when the readers approach the lectern to read a portion of scripture, or the priest reads from the Gospel and then bends low to kiss the book, or as he sets the eucharistic table. These moments of silence have become some of my favorite parts of the Mass. There's an anticipation in the air as worshippers prepare for the next thing, and with a formal order of worship to the service, they know what's coming. God has worked on me in these spaces, breaking down misgivings I've had about traditions other than my own. A divine truth has settled inside of me—Jesus can be found among us. It's not about the labels we like to assign one another: progressive, conservative, complementarian, egalitarian, Protestant, Catholic, Orthodox. It's about gathering together and meeting with God. Whether in a remote place, on a busy street in a large city, by yourself, or seated among the faithful, God longs to create that quiet space in our souls, where he can speak.

CHAPTER 5

A Reflection on Elijah

O Lord, God of Abraham, Isaac, and Israel, let it be known this day that you are God in Israel, that I am your servant, and that I have done all these things at your bidding. Answer me, O Lord, answer me, so that this people may know that you, O Lord, are God, and that you have turned their hearts back.

—1 Kings 18:36–37

There are any number of ways to interact with scripture. I'm convinced part of the reason more of us aren't students of the Bible is that we haven't been taught to do this well, and on those occasions where we do make the attempt, we read it in the same old way we always have, finding it dry and boring. Have you ever read scripture out of a sense of obligation? May it never be so. "Indeed, the word of God is living and active, sharper than any two-edged sword, piercing until it divides soul from spirit, joints from marrow; is able to judge the intentions of the heart" (Hebrews 4:12). That sounds anything but dry and boring.

Writing a book on spiritual practices means I'm going to offer a fair amount of scripture. I thought it might be helpful to draw back the curtain and show you methods I've learned to embark on a lifelong journey of reading God's word. To show you how I study. Here's the process I followed as I looked at the life of the prophet Elijah, whose faith had both shaky and steadfast times in it. Basically showing us, he was human like you and me.

When I write about stories in the Bible, I often find I don't know what wisdom I am gleaning until I write my thoughts down. This should not come as a surprise, as it's how I process most of the thoughts I have. As a writer, I don't know what I think about something until I write it out. Maybe you're like that, too, or maybe you comprehend better when you read out loud. Reading "silently" to ourselves is a rather modern invention; for centuries, those who could read, read out loud, even when alone. Give it a try—you may be surprised by what you "hear" differently. Sometimes in reading a passage from the Bible, it helps to read a whole book in one setting or at least to read the chapters before and after the section you're reading. Context makes a difference, and so can placing yourself into the narrative (all practices we'll learn more about in this book). Are you part of the crowd, wondering at the strong words of a prophet, or a member of one of the first house churches, hearing Timothy preach? Whatever you can do to interact with the story will help you to better see it in your imagination.

■ ■ ■

Method: Here was my process for thinking through the stories we have about Elijah. As I go along, I keep a notebook nearby for my questions and discoveries. I first had to flip through the two books of Kings to remember which stories belong to the prophet Elijah, and which stories are about Elisha. I'm always getting them confused in my mind. In writing about silence for this book, I recalled a story about one of them hearing God in the quiet and wanted to refresh my mind on the details. (The story I was thinking about is in the nineteenth chapter of 1 Kings, found about a third of the way through the Old Testament.)

Next, I considered the context surrounding the story. Being in 1 Kings, we find ourselves pretty early in the monarchy stage of Israel's history. The nation of Israel has split into two kingdoms: the northern (Israel) and the southern (Judah). Elijah was a prophet during the reign of King Ahab and Queen Jezebel, who were bad

leaders. These facts meant a lot of turmoil, which helps us understand how Elijah could get so drained that he ran off to the wilderness. It's exhausting feeling like you're the only one trying to live a
righteous life. We don't read of Elijah having many companions.

Here is where my reflection on Elijah ended up:

In the books of Kings we meet Elijah, a hairy man who wore a
leather belt around his waist (2 Kings 1:8). As I've already confessed, I
often get Elijah and Elisha confused. When I mentioned this on Twitter, several people suggested remembering the order based on the
alphabetical "j" in Elijah and "s" in Elisha. Another man, who is Jewish
and lives in Jerusalem, responded (see why social media is awesome?),
pointing out the original Hebrew names are Eliyahu and Elisha. I jot-
ted this down in my Bible and know it will help with my mix-ups.

When we meet Elijah in chapter seventeen of 1 Kings, he pre-
dicts a drought. God promises to care for him during this time, however, and in this opening scene he instructs Elijah to hide by Wadi
Cherith (some translations use brook or creek), drinking water from
the wadi and eating bread and meat brought to him by ravens.

Another time, God asks Elijah to visit a widow from Zara-
phath, who was running out of food. He performs a miracle, filling
her jar with meal and her jug with oil, so her family could eat for
many days. Some time later, the widow's son dies, and Elijah raises
him from the dead. With the land still suffering from a drought,
Elijah later goes head-to-head with the priests of Baal, praying God
would bring fire to the altar he built. After building an altar, he digs
a trench around it. He places wood on the altar and cuts a bull in
pieces. He orders four pitchers of water to be poured on the burnt
offering and on the wood. Three times he commands this. The
water overflows and fills the trench. Then he prays for fire to ignite
the sacrifice, calling on the God of Abraham, Isaac, and Israel. God
answers that prayer, and more, when he sends fire down, consum-
ing the burnt offering, the wood, the stones, the dust, and any
remaining water in the trench around the altar.

God did great, even miraculous, things in Elijah's life. King
Ahab and Queen Jezebel were not impressed. Or maybe they were

impressed and felt threatened. When Jezebel sent a message of doom to Elijah, he developed a case of spiritual amnesia, forgetting all God had done. All Elijah could see were the immediate circumstances set before him. Scripture tells us he was afraid, and he fled.

Elijah walked a day's journey into the wilderness, finally sitting down under a broom tree. He asked God to take his life.

And then he fell asleep. God gave him rest, and with rest we often get a fresh perspective. Two times an angel comes, touches Elijah, speaks words of comfort to him, and offers nourishment in the form of a cake baked on a stone and a jar of water. What Elijah received from this messenger of God was enough to walk for forty days and forty nights to a place called Horeb, identified elsewhere as Mount Sinai. This is the place where God made the Mosaic covenant with Israel.

There, Elijah finds a cave, and he goes to sleep. His circumstances haven't changed much, but God keeps showing up. The Lord asks Elijah what he's doing at Horeb. Elijah pleads his case: I have been zealous for you, now they're seeking my life.

Elijah wasn't sure God would protect him from Ahab and Jezebel, so he ran away and is now wandering in the wilderness. What is God's response? You might want to sit down for this.

> He said, "Go out and stand on the mountain before the Lord, for the Lord is about to pass by." Now there was a great wind, so strong that it was splitting mountains and breaking rocks in pieces before the Lord, but the Lord was not in the wind; and after the wind an earthquake, but the Lord was not in the earthquake; and after the earthquake a fire, but the Lord was not in the fire; and after the fire a sound of sheer silence. (1 Kings 19:11–12)

It was at this moment Elijah finally stopped running. Again, his circumstances hadn't changed, God had never left, but Elijah could finally sense the presence of God in the sheer silence. A few verses later, Elijah sets out from there, and he does as God instructs him to do. He finds Elisha and makes him prophet in his place.

God is so patient with us. He is active in our lives. On occasion, we even get to glimpse miracles. He seeks us out, nourishes us, and wants to hear what we have to say. In all of this, I'm convinced his favorite moments, whether out of desperation or discipline, are when he has us all to himself. When we're alone with God, and we shut out the noise of the world (wind and earthquakes and fire, oh my), we find him in the sheer silence.

This sheer silence is where his presence shines the brightest and shapes us to be more like him. Take a moment to focus on the place where Elijah eventually met with God. A cave. We know them to be dark, damp, and cold. The farther in you go, the harder it is to see the way back out. I've been in a few caves, and I'm usually sharing the space with a cauldron of bats. Without proper lighting or a tour guide, caves can be downright scary. We don't know what Elijah's cave looked like, or how far into it he traveled, but we can use our imaginations to better understand the scene. The isolation we feel in our metaphorical caves can be equally daunting. Sometimes it might seem like the last place to find the peace of God. Yet, time and time again, we hear stories of people who do receive that very peace that passes all understanding in the midst of their cave experience. God draws near in a way words can hardly describe.

A handful of times over the years, my world has gone shaky with a health scare. Most recently, an ultrasound showed a tiny nodule in my throat, and my doctor didn't like the shape of it. He encouraged me to have a needle biopsy done, saying if it was his wife or mother, he'd want to have it checked out. I scheduled the appointment for later that month. Then I waited. I asked a few friends to pray and talked with my mom and husband about my concerns. Mostly, though, I handled the unknown internally. I didn't want opinions. I surely wasn't going to google it, because we wouldn't know anything until the test results came back anyway. The day of the appointment, no one went with me. I drove home in silence. Even though I looked to be alone, God was there. I threw out prayers to him all along the way. He calmed me. Fortunately, this time, the spot was benign. I'm thankful, so thankful, when we need our worlds to go silent, to deal with something on our own, God speaks into those times.

Will you pray with me?

God, we long for a word from you. Still our minds and hearts to prepare room for you to speak. However you choose to interact with us, may we be ready to dwell in your presence, to listen and obey. Amen.

CHAPTER 6

Is God Silent?

Behind the depressing silence of this sea, the silence of God . . . the feeling that while men raise their voices in anguish God remains with folded arms, silent.

—Shūsaku Endō, *Silence*

t's an age-old question. When unspeakable things happen in our own lives or around the world, where is God? Fortunately, we have things like history and various genres of books to explore topics like this, perhaps without having to learn some of life's hardest lessons for ourselves.

We also know of men and women who, over the years, have felt led by God to make a departure from society. Cloisters of those who have taken religious orders exist around the world. Often, people seek out these devout individuals or groups for prayers, wisdom, and guidance on their own path. What unique things might they have to teach us?

In the examples we'll consider here, the people of God have intentionally gone to remote places and chosen hard lives away from the conveniences they would have found in society. We can learn a great deal from their lifestyles of silence.

In 2016, the movie *Silence*, a film based on a 1966 book with the same name, was released. I saw it mentioned all over my social media feeds. Companion books were written about it. Suddenly, silence became a trending topic.

Silence shows up throughout this historical fiction novel written by Shūsaku Endō (I read a translated English version). In the seventeenth century, two Jesuit priests from Portugal go to Japan. They want to minister to the local Catholic Church presence there, and to find their mentor, Priest Ferreira, to learn whether or not he has apostatized (the abandonment of one's faith). Upon arrival, they find the Christians have gone underground, hiding from authorities. Some of the most beautiful scenes from the book are of the arrival of priests after many years without one. The people held Mass at night, deep in the woods so they wouldn't be caught, but finally they could gather for worship with a shepherd among their flock. Many church-related things we take for granted become part of these Christians' lives again: there were baptisms, the Eucharist was celebrated, and people were able to attend confession. The priests struggle with the choices they're forced to make, though, between serving the people and leaving them so they would not be discovered, thus protecting the converts from torture at the hands of government officials. The book shares many of the prayers and contemplative images Priest Rodrigues exercises to help him endure the days and months of solitude. The book also raises an important question.

What do we do when it feels like God has gone silent in our circumstances? Eventually, the two priests are separated and Father Rodrigues is thrown in prison. He doesn't know what happened to his ministry partner. While imprisoned, the officials began torturing the Christians around him, and rather than killing the priest himself, which seemed to strengthen the new Christians, the Japanese officials tortured the people, making the priest and other believers watch. Every time, they cried out to God, and God did not seem to respond.

Father Rodrigues endures this for months, and one of his main mechanisms for coping is to envision himself with Jesus at the cross in the hours of his arrest and crucifixion. This gives him some semblance of comfort and resolve. Here is one such time:

> He simply closed his eyes and thought of the Stations of the
> Cross, one by one, now being prayed at some monastery; and

he kept moving his dry tongue as he tried to mutter the words
of the prayers . . .

When this man had gone out through the gate of the
Temple up the sloping path to Golgotha bearing his cross,
struggling for every step and reeling as he walked, the swelling
mob, all agog with curiosity, had followed after him. "Women
of Jerusalem, weep not for me but for yourselves and for your
children. For the day will come." These words came up in his
mind. Many centuries ago, that man tasted with his dried
and swollen tongue all the suffering that I now endure, he
reflected. And this sense of suffering shared softly eased his
mind and heart more than the sweetest water.

We all have contended with similar questions. Our family has
friends who have one biological child, but then were unable to
have more of their own. They've offered foster care to a number
of children over the years, wanting to move forward with adoption
when circumstances allowed for that. It's a messy, slow process that
comes with a good deal of heartache. Another couple we know
signed on with an adoption agency and were identified as a match,
with the adoption going through quickly. Who decides what is best
for the orphaned among us? Where is God in all the waiting? Why
do these things sometimes happen quickly, and other times drag
on for years, if they happen at all?

In *Silence*, where was God when the priest and Japanese
Christians were suffering? The priest answered it this way: myste-
riously God was by their side, suffering with them, and this mat-
tered more than anything the priests or the people experienced.
Rather than answers, God gave them divine comfort by making
his presence known.

For most of us, our shaky ground is not anything like the
persecution these priests and Japanese Christians experienced
in the seventeenth century. There are lessons we can take with
us from their experience, though. As much as they could, the
people gathered together. They worshipped together whenever

and wherever possible, although much of their faith was practiced in government-imposed seclusion. Faith has tremendous sustaining power if we rely on it. They came to rely on the fact; in Christ, no one is ever truly alone.

■ ■ ■

In her book *The Wild Land Within: Cultivating Wholeness through Spiritual Practice*, Lisa Colón DeLay introduces her readers to fourth-century Egyptian desert father Evagrius Ponticus. The desert fathers and mothers were a group of Christians who settled in the Egyptian desert and lived there as hermits, focusing on praying and reading the psalms. Their writings are readily available on the internet and in various books today. Evagrius recognized that wise disciples had apatheia. DeLay defines this as "a state of calm, which is the prerequisite for love and knowledge." Where do you think these desert fathers and mothers developed a state of calm, this ability to remove rash reactions from their behavior? Silence, with God. Having removed themselves from society, these men and women were often viewed as guides by those who came to them for insight and prayer. As DeLay notes, "Evagrius advises that making wisdom manifest happens by taking on the nature of Christ through imitation and submission. This eventually results in an even-tempered disciple whose life is centered in God's way and will. This is a life that bears the fruit of the Holy Spirit." Imitating Christ, an even-tempered disciple. I've known a few men and women like this, although they did not set themselves apart from society. They're often older, having weathered many storms and emerged faithful. They almost glow like Moses, and I could sit in their presence in, well, silence for great lengths of time. This is who I long to be. Meeting God in the solitude will form these character traits in us.

What Endō wrote about in *Silence*, what Evagrius found in the desert, and what DeLay shares with readers in her own book is the mutual concept of becoming more Christlike by thinking on

Christ, imitating Christ, and submitting to Christ's instructive wisdom. This is why we seek out spiritual practices, even though we're still very much a part of society, to place ourselves humbly before Christ on a regular basis.

We often give up on spiritual practices because they don't seem to give us adequate answers to our most difficult questions, and we struggle to see the difference they are making in our lives. These are not practices intended to provide straightforward answers or immediate results, but to make us increasingly aware of God's presence. Quick fixes—perhaps satisfying in the short run—are always there, beckoning to us when we need a pick-me-up. Building a lifestyle of faith cannot be rushed, but God is faithful and wants to reveal himself. The slow, steady work of showing up, being present to God as God is present to us is one way we can experience God's ongoing grace in our lives. Grace that plants us on solid ground, again and again.

PART II

STABILITY

CHAPTER 7

Faith in Its Fullness

The kingdom we are to root ourselves in, however, is not one of self-fulfillment or privatization but one that nurtures the self-forgetting life.

—Tara Beth Leach, *Radiant Church*

Ours is an individualistic society. From an early age, parents teach their children to be self-reliant, sometimes to the detriment of their relationships with others. Sometimes this can even be a barrier to our reliance on God. We can convince ourselves that asking for help is a sign of weakness. We're taught to stuff away emotions perceived as negative, such as sadness, loneliness, or anger, learning instead to focus on finding ways to make ourselves happy. Perhaps that is why we're so drawn to more rapid remedies, in order to numb our emotions. In much of life, we develop an "every person for themselves" mentality.

Yet the kingdom of God is the polar opposite of that. Work on the harmful effects of the individualism we've internalized is one of the first things Christ wants to undo in us. My favorite kind of humor is a well-delivered sarcastic remark. In the proper context, I find snark funny. You know where sarcasm and snark almost never fit? In building safe relationships with one another. I've learned this one the hard way. If we are going to help people overcome their individualistic tendencies, and trust us enough to ask for help, to admit weakness, to ask hard questions and share feelings, we've got to be direct and loving. There's a connection too with being able to trust those in our lives, and how much we determine we can trust God. If we are going to overcome our own individualistic tendencies and trust another person and God enough to ask for help, to admit weakness, to ask hard questions and share feelings, we need to find that same sense of safety in relationship.

It's in the twelfth chapter of First Corinthians Paul talks about being the body of Christ. This is one of my favorite metaphors used to describe us as Christ-followers. He follows this idea up with what many recognize as the love chapter. Although we often hear the thirteenth chapter of First Corinthians at weddings, it was written as a descriptive for the behavior members of the church at Corinth, and every church since, should exhibit. Our love should not be a noisy gong or a clanging cymbal.

Rather, here's what love within the body of Christ looks like:

Love is patient; love is kind; love is not envious or boastful or arrogant or rude. It does not insist on its own way; it is not irritable or resentful; it does not rejoice in wrongdoing, but rejoices in the truth. It bears all things, believes all things, hopes all things, endures all things. Love never ends. (1 Corinthians 13:4–8a)

Christianity is never about us alone. As Christ-followers, whether or not we find ourselves part of a regular worshipping congregation, we are members of the body of Christ. Our faith actually has fluidity to it, flowing back and forth between individual practice and communal involvement. "For just as the body is one and has many members, and all the members of the body, though many, are one body, so it is with Christ" (1 Corinthians 12:12).

Think how weird it would be to see an eyeball walking around on its own. This is how silly it's become in my mind that we would put man-made limitations on which of Jesus's followers are in the body, and which ones aren't. Is it complicated? You bet. Are we still one body of Christ? We are. Is an individual a part of the body if they've stopped attending church for any number of reasons? Paul seems to think so. "If the foot would say, 'Because I am not a hand, I do not belong to the body,' that would not make it any less a part of the body" (1 Corinthians 12:15).

When I spend time being intentionally aware of God's presence, I'm a better member of the body of Christ. I partner better with the members of my local church and I'm a better representative in the community and online. As the Spirit makes lasting changes in me, it should be evident to everyone I come into contact with, and not just every person, but the very world we live in. Ultimately, God's redemption includes all of God's creatures, and this planet we live on, and when I'm attuned to how God is at work in the world, creation care becomes all-encompassing.

When you think about it, we're receiving quite an invitation. To commune with God, with one another, and have this all work in tandem to make us exactly who God fashioned us to be. I attended a contemplative prayer class once, and as I was answering a question about the connection I made with God through an exercise, I had a breakthrough moment, and blurted out, "It's like magic." Immediately, I was embarrassed. The instructor responded graciously, "It's OK. It is kind of like that." Or divine revelation—God at work in us and through us—which is even better than magic.

As we consider the practices we can use to draw near to God, you'll find a big variety. They come from a number of traditions, almost as if God designed it this way to encourage us to learn from one another. Prayerfully consider what practices will lead you into a deeper relationship with Jesus. What practices help you step out of an individualistic mindset? As human beings, we're always changing: getting older, facing new circumstances, experiencing life changes, stepping into a new role in the body of Christ. Regardless of where you find yourself now, in five years, or in ten years, spiritual practices journey with you. They'll change along the way too.

It's also helpful to realize we rarely follow one spiritual practice at a time. Sometimes while I sit in silence, my thoughts turn into prayer. I can lament and praise God in a breath prayer (inhale, lament; exhale, praise). I read a psalm and suddenly I'm lamenting, praying, and singing all at the same time. From the earliest days of the Bible, poetry flowed into scripture, which flowed into the church's hymns, creeds, and confessions. Keep in mind, too, that these practices are never for your benefit alone. As you participate, the Spirit makes you less self-centered and more Christlike, benefiting all of us.

When my husband and I take a car ride to wherever, we don't always do the same thing. Sometimes we sit in silence. He might turn on an audiobook he's listening to and I'll read my book or put in earbuds. The times we do talk, it's some of our best conversations. Something about sitting side by side, not staring at an electronic device, with the open road ahead of us, makes for good talk time. Whatever we end up doing as we travel, it's a safe space because I'm with someone I love and trust.

That's what God longs for with us. It's not a formula: fifteen minutes reading a devotion, five minutes in silence (staring at my watch), praying to wrap it all up. The list of what we call spiritual practices is limitless if we invite Jesus to join us in the activities. What I do in my walk with God today might not look like how I do things tomorrow. Sometimes we do certain spiritual practices for a season, and the Holy Spirit can be a faithful guide here. The majority of my mornings, I read my Bible chronologically. Genesis to Revelation, with set readings for each day. I do this in a group online, so there is a fluidity here too. Am I reading for myself, or reading, sharing, and gathering insight with those in our group?

Before I read chapters in my Bible each day, I read something brief. It might be a short piece from a book of poetry, a devotional that is a few paragraphs in length, or a formal prayer from a prayer book. I rotate through various books based on what my spirit is calling for at any given time. While I've learned there is a benefit to reading the same prayers on a daily basis, I've found it beneficial to read alongside different church traditions, joining up with brothers and sisters in Christ around the world.

The ways to pray are limitless too, for it's simply talking to God. We have any number of ways to read the Bible, for it's simply getting to know God.

A growing faith has a fluidity to it. Eventually, all the good work God has been doing in you is going to pour out. When I'm spiritually filled up, I'm a more stable, grounded person. I serve God better in my church because I've spent time in God's word throughout the week. I'm gentler with my family because I started my day sitting still in the presence of the Holy Spirit, who cultivates the fruit of gentleness in me. God brings to mind people who would be there to help me when life gets hard; all I have to do is ask. I think on who I could help as well.

■ ■ ■

This might seem like a strange place to include a section on the Sermon on the Mount (Matthew 5–7), but I assure you it is not. We studied this passage one fall in Bible study, using Sandra Glahn's workbook *Mocha on the Mount* to guide our conversation. As I often do, I supplemented my teaching with some additional resources. I read Dallas Willard's *The Divine Conspiracy* and Oswald Chambers's *Studies in the Sermon on the Mount*. Looking back, I was crazy to think we could cover Jesus's famous sermon in six to eight weeks.

Our conversation ranged from metaphorical understandings to literal instruction, and every thread seemed to take us back to the same root—right living in the eyes of God requires a right heart. In the beatitudes, who is blessed? Those who are going about the business of their father in heaven. I was taught the list of beatitudes showcased character traits we should aspire to: poor in spirit, those who mourn, the meek, those who hunger and thirst for righteousness, the merciful, the pure in heart, the peacemakers, and those who are persecuted for righteousness' sake. I heard a sermon once that noted the list as be-attitudes that progress as a person deepens in their relationship with Christ. That's a compelling way to read it. In his book, Willard looked at each quality as a personality type, pointing to the fact that God made us the way we are, and there's room for each of us in God's kingdom. In our group, we wondered which personality type we might be. Those in the Mennonite tradition see these teachings as the core of Christianity, and they developed their understanding of pacifism in part from this sermon text. Understanding how other people and church traditions viewed the truths in this sermon served as a good reminder that we learn from the Bible in community, even when we're not face-to-face. We read with the men or women who translated the text, with whatever study notes or commentaries or books or articles we reference, with our cultural lens, and with anyone we discuss the Bible with in actual conversation.

Moving into the sermon passages on anger, adultery, divorce, oaths, retaliation, and enemies, our group had a number of interesting conversations. Churches over the years have taken some strong stances based on their understanding of Jesus's teachings here. Among the women in our group, we kept sharing our very human stories and kept coming back to the spiritual health of our hearts before a holy God. As we wrapped up our study, we realized a group could continue studying these three chapters for years to come. Jesus could preach a good sermon. We were in agreement with the crowd, "Now when Jesus had finished saying these things, the crowds were astounded at his teaching, for he taught them as one having authority, and not as their scribes" (Matthew 7:28–29).

Another area of fluidity we'll explore in this book is the intersection of prayer and scripture. This is definitely an area where we can learn in community: in classrooms, small groups, or with workbooks. I'll save the psalms for later but here, I want to tell you about a prayer experience I signed up for, dividing my time between individual and group practice, while writing this book.

I had the opportunity to pursue a longtime dream: a silent retreat. In looking for a retreat center, I found a number of options, with various church affiliations, near my home, and I chose a Franciscan center for prayer. Sitting on fifty acres, the space is set apart as holy ground. Wildlife roams freely, all is quiet, the food was delicious and plentiful, there were plenty of places to settle in alone and pray. I've no doubt Saint Francis would have approved of the grounds and the variety of places to have times of focused prayer. After I decided on this small retreat center in the Chicago area, I checked their calendar to see if there were any events happening during my stay. My first full day, a psychologist, who was also a lay Jesuit, held a workshop on imaginative prayer in the style of St. Ignatius, a Catholic priest who founded the Jesuit order in the sixteenth century in Spain (Ignatius also brought us the Examen, mentioned earlier). This workshop felt like a bonus.

Perhaps my favorite part of the workshop was that imaginative prayer didn't feel new, I just hadn't realized there was a name for it. I'd long been putting myself into the stories I read in scripture, imagining the details of the scenes in order to make them seem more real, considering the experience of each person in the story. Our workshop teacher gave us two passages of scripture to consider: Jesus walking on the water and the parable of the good Samaritan. Each time, he read the passage for our group, then sent us off with a short packet to complete on our own. We were instructed to read the passages multiple times, asking God to help us consider the passage with our imagination—a method he called contemplation—rather than our mind. Then, go to the scene. Using all five senses, consider each character in the story, where the story takes place, what actions transpire. At this point, pray about what God would have you experience. What's something you might have missed about the passage before? Does God want to say something specifically to you in this time together?

In looking more closely at this exercise, I wondered what the difference was between contemplation and meditation. The former word is new to me, the latter I've come to associate with new age spirituality. Yet I see it referenced often in Christian books and workshops. A friend who is affiliated with the Carmelite Nuns of

Great Britain helped me understand the difference. "Meditation helps us still ourselves and brings us to focus on God," she wrote. "Contemplation is 'just being' in the presence of God." I've found both are utilized in these prayer exercises.

At the main building of the retreat center, I went downstairs to pray through our first assigned passage. I'd heard there was a chapel down there but hadn't seen it yet. I must have made a wrong turn, because I ended up in the laundry room, where there was a couch and table along the wall. I listened to the washing machine going through a cycle as I read about Jesus calming the storm. It seemed appropriate background noise. I sat and took in my surroundings, feeling a quietness settle around me.

We were assigned Matthew 14:22–33 for this prayer exercise. Earlier in the day, Jesus had been teaching a crowd. He dismissed the people and told the disciples to go ahead of him in a boat. Then, Jesus went off on his own to pray, and although we aren't told specifics regarding time, we do read that Jesus didn't go to join the disciples until right before dawn. Many of us know what a storm is like on open water, with rough waves and a mighty wind. The disciples were in the throes of it and had been for some time. As each member of our group thought through the story, we filled out two worksheets: one identifying each character in the story, and another with five questions to help us identify how we felt as we read the story. The first question on this page was, "Which character do you identify with?" After I'd completed the worksheet, I spent the final solitary moments sitting before God, contemplating the role he plays in calming the storms of life.

When our group came back together, the facilitator asked each of us who we had listed as character we identified with the most. Oftentimes when praying through these stories, one particular point or turn of phrase or mental image might strike you as significant. Then, if you use imaginative prayer to contemplate the story at a later time, something entirely different might seem like the most important thing God has for you that time around. That day, I identified with Jesus because I know that feeling of needing to decompress after being in a crowd, teaching and giving of yourself. He didn't seem to have any misgivings about sending the disciples off in the boat. I'm also learning it's healthy to take this time away. We likely won't miss anything major, and we can join up with the group at a later time, refreshed. While imaginative prayer does not require a group setting or the conversation that followed our group's time of contemplation, it was interesting hearing the different perspectives. We bring our individual selves to the discussion, but the group dynamics play a role too.

When continuing this practice later on my own, I kept in mind the perspectives we had shared that day together. I thought on how the character we relate to is influenced by a number of factors: where we are emotionally, what we're dealing with in daily life, our personalities, what we had for breakfast. Does a meek and mild person ever relate to the bold and spontaneous Peter? Each time I have done this exercise, it seemed to bring up new parts of a story I hadn't considered before. Something about honing in on the details of a few verses better puts me in the scene. Reading about what happened just before and just after the story you're reading helps with this as well. The men and women were like us. This sounds obvious, but when you smell the fish cooking, feel water from the Sea of Galilee splash over your feet, observe the crowds moving ever closer to Jesus, something changes. You realize the Bible is not only a book, it's a revelation that brings a divine presence to everyday things. Through these pages, we can better know God, and the imperfect people he uses when they fully give their lives to him.

Our next exercise was contemplating the parable of the good Samaritan. Luke is the only writer who shares this story. It is another scene that's easy to imagine. Again, our group heard the story and then spent time alone, reflecting on the parable, listing the characters in the story and their primary action. When asked who I identified with, my answer again surprised me. It was that kind of prayer day, I guess. I noted the parting instructions the Samaritan had for the innkeeper, before leaving the injured man in his care. "Look after him," he said.

Keep in mind, part of the reason I went on this prayer retreat was to quiet my mind, reflect on the ideas in this book, and have uninterrupted writing time. We tend to focus on the Samaritan, but the innkeeper played a key supporting role. He hadn't come upon the scene of the accident. We don't know his religious affiliation or his ethnicity. My mind went to another famous innkeeper in the gospels, the one in Bethlehem the night Jesus was born, with no room in his or her inn for the holy family. What do innkeepers have to teach us about welcoming outsiders? How often do we come across people after they've already been robbed and beaten up? We didn't see it happen, and we weren't the first responders, but the wounds are there. That day of my workshop, Jesus echoed the words of the good Samaritan, "Look after him." And he was talking to me.

I thought of people who spend a great deal of their life on shaky ground. For some of us, the bottom drops out at church, when we realize our gifts, perhaps our very selves, aren't accepted. The phrase "Look after him" jumped off the page of my bible. When we came back together as a group to discuss what our time with Jesus had been like, I was still hearing the phrase. I mentioned being drawn to the innkeeper's role in the story, an individual who knew little about what had happened or how it came about that the Samaritan had brought an injured man to his inn. As I told the group that day, we often don't know the situation of marginalized people who come to us either. We don't know what they've been robbed of, how they might be broken, and sometimes their wounds aren't even visible. When we find them placed in our care, whether we're being paid or not, Jesus instructs us to do what the innkeeper was asked to do. "Look after him." Have mercy.

As I mentioned, imaginative prayer comes naturally to me, but that's not the case for everyone. It was a difficult task for those in my group who were more analytical. Much of it depends on how you're wired. Try putting yourself in the context of the Bible story, even if it feels unnatural, as it might get easier with practice. Think of the actions for each character in the story.

Realize you don't have to use this as your only form of prayer, or even in the rotation of prayers. I asked our workshop instructor how he decided on a prayer method when he sat down to spend time with God. His response was, "I ask God what he would have me to do that time."

During the next day of this prayer retreat, I tried another new-to-me method of silent prayer. Walking a labyrinth is an ancient prayer activity. The prayer center had one on the grounds, so I thought I'd try it. A brochure outside the beginning of the space explains this particular labyrinth is a replica of one found in the floor of Chartres Cathedral in France, constructed around 1220 CE. From the brochure: "A labyrinth is an ancient circular diagram found in many cultures around the world. In its classical form, this sacred diagram consists of a single concentric path with no possibility of going astray." It's not a maze, meant to confuse the participant, but rather a way for individuals to put their feet to praying, alongside their spirit. A labyrinth represents our spiritual life, which is a winding road. Consider what questions you have for God as you stand at the labyrinth's entrance. As you walk, whatever comes to mind, examine it, reflect on it prayerfully, and capture it or release it. Many find the repetition of a word to be helpful as they walk. As I walked this labyrinth, a vibrant yellow maple tree catching my eye around every bend, I thought about the beautiful things God has created, including his Church and our practices. God knows my misgivings, my feelings of ineptitude in writing about spiritual disciplines, when most days I feel as if the concept is entirely new to me too. God reminded me then, and keeps reminding me, that we've been walking together a long time. All he wants from me is obedience—whose root word means "to listen deeply," after all—and that means sharing with you what I've learned. I pray we can keep learning together.

Walking the labyrinth at the prayer center that day brought me back to the only other labyrinth I've seen in person, just a few months prior, so I offered up a prayer for those I'd been with that day as well. My friend Ellie was giving us a tour of her home. In the center of her backyard, flat rocks weave their way around in an intricate, circular path. The story goes that Ellie's husband was scheduled to have surgery. It was a highly stressful time for their family, and she needed to find a way to release some of the angst. She also desperately wanted a place set aside where she could pray. She had a number of large pieces of rock delivered, dumped in a large pile in her backyard. At various times during that season of their lives, she'd grab a hammer and spend time doing manual labor out among the Michigan pines surrounding their property. This outlet gave her a place to physically work out her fears and anxiety in the fresh air outdoors. Sometimes physical activity takes on the form of prayer. Since constructing her own labyrinth, Ellie has prayed in this space a number of times. I did not walk her labyrinth that day. There was a group of us, and we had stopped by on our way to lunch. I didn't know I'd have another opportunity so soon. I sensed God wanted me to give it a try. After doing this kind of prayer walk myself, I could see it being a good exercise to do with others too, and talk about your experience afterward.

The walking itself is a big benefit: getting fresh air, moving your body. It forces you to slow down and yet keep moving. Praying while walking a labyrinth has been shown to initiate what health professionals call the "relaxation response," which may help slow down one's breathing, reduce tension in muscles, and lower blood pressure. I read an essay once, written by a woman who had taken up body building. She used the repetitions done with each exercise to give structure to her prayer, much like a breath prayer. While working out, she could feel the strength of her body, and over time felt it getting stronger. She praised God for making her strong and capable. Releasing endorphins during the workout, she felt better mentally and physically. I've given some thought to the benefits of engaging our bodies with our prayer life. Taking the body along on the prayer journey is like going on mini-pilgrimages, offering a number of health benefits while connecting to God and those who join us at the same time. There are many elements that come together to form a full and healthy faith life, and they all flow together in a beautiful and sacred way.

CHAPTER 8

Make Me a Better Pray-er

I'd pray but I think I already am, always.

—Sarah Bessey, *Field Notes* newsletter

n 2015, southwest Michigan had some shaky ground, literally. It was the largest quake in Michigan since 1947. I was at the local gas station, getting out of my car to go inside, when the ground shifted a little and my car door shook. It wasn't significant, and no damage was done to our home, but I felt an undeniable tremor for a few moments. I'd never experienced an earthquake before, and although small, it left me somewhat unsettled. If it had been a bigger earthquake, like the ones others experience around the world, I would have found my way to a safe spot, hit my knees, and started praying. It's true in life too. Sometimes things go off-kilter and we seek to weather those changes with confidence. Other times, what starts out small turns into a catastrophe. We need spiritual rhythms in place to help us through these situations. Prayer helps with both instances, and everything in between. The psalmist encourages us, "Cast your burden on the Lord, and he will sustain you; he will never permit the righteous to be moved" (Psalm 55:22).

I always told myself I wasn't good at prayer. Those stories about monks praying multiple times a day, and people waking up at four thirty in the morning to pray for a few hours before the rest of the house was up for the day? The only thing I do at four thirty in the morning is sleep.

Prayer is not about formulas or right and wrong ways. Talk and listen, listen and talk. This is the entire point of the psalms: prayers and petitions on behalf of individuals and gatherings of people. Most days, I get more from listening to what I sense God is telling me than from talking myself. It's in these nonverbal times I often hear what God would have me do, and then when I go about doing those things, especially if they require a great deal of courage, I can proceed with a divine bravery. Maybe you struggle with knowing if it's God telling you to do something, or your own impulses. We can all do this at times. Try not to be in a hurry when you're seeking an answer in your prayers. God's direction will come with a certain amount of peace, even if the task ahead is difficult. Confirmation might also come from scripture or someone you know to be trustworthy. Those times when God doesn't respond with a clear response, I've learned to wait on him, knowing he is a faithful guide, even if things don't always happen on my timing.

When we're doing the talking part of praying, we can pray spontaneously, or we can recite prayers familiar as a soft blanket wrapped around us on the first brisk mornings of autumn. We can use books with formal prayers. We can use published prayers. We can pray using scripture. Discovering ways to pray throughout our days, throughout our lives, can provide a solid foundation, no matter what we end up facing. Even if, like me, you don't consider yourself to be good at prayer, there are no wrong ways or wrong times to start. It's not a competition; whatever way you choose to pray will please God.

For me, prayer begins in the first few minutes after I wake up. I tell God good morning. We note the change in seasons: it's staying dark longer, look at the sunrise, gonna be a hot one today. From there, the conversation continues all day long. It's less about set times of prayer. God and I talk all the time.

One way God continuously offers me words of wisdom is in a repeated phrase I'll hear internally during particular times of my life. These aren't words I've thought up myself, but they are brought to the surface in my mind. They too turn into prayer. Earlier, I shared about a time this happened as we settled into our current home. More than once, God impressed the phrase "you'll heal here" on my mind. Another time, I was struggling with where I was headed as a mom, as a wife, and as a writer. I wondered if I was moving forward in a right direction. One Sunday, walking forward in the communion line at church, I internally heard the words "trust and obey." This phrase came with a calm assurance that God would continue to guide me, even though I could not see the way ahead clearly. My response was obedience, as I understood it. Here's another phrase I have heard, "Trust the process." It has served as a reminder that doing anything worthwhile is going to take a while. These phrases feel like part of my ongoing prayer conversation with God. You may also, in the quiet or in the bustle of life, hear a word you need. Perhaps not. Perhaps your conversation with God will take a more active twist, with opportunities presenting themselves, or situations suddenly feeling untenable. I pray you will know the sound of God's voice when it comes to you, however it may come to you.

■ ■ ■

There is biblical testimony that God's people have traditionally set aside specific times to pray and you may find that to be a helpful pattern in your life. The sixth chapter of the book of Daniel tells of Daniel's unfortunate run-in with the lions' den. After King Darius decreed that anyone who prays to any god or human other than the king himself for thirty days would be thrown in with the lions, we read Daniel's response: "Although Daniel knew that the document had been signed, he continued to go to his house, which had windows in its upper room open toward Jerusalem, and to get down on his knees three times a day to pray to his God and praise him, just as he had done previously" (Daniel 6:10). The Psalms also remind us that "seven times a day I praise you" (Psalm 119:164a). The ancient tradition of prayer referred to here shows the psalmist prayed at set times, from before dawn through to bedtime.

I'd read about this practice, known as "praying the hours," in a number of books and decided starting my day this way in particular appealed to me. If I'm honest, those spiritual practices that involve reading and praying words always feel the most comfortable to me. "Liturgy of the hours" is a way of expressing the more formal practice of praying at specific times throughout the day.

When I start the coffee maker, I have approximately five minutes to read while it percolates. I find these shorter reads set before me an efficacious picture of what the day might bring. This might be partly from the words, but also from the lyrical composition. Reading a formal prayer (or sometimes a poem), I praise God for giving authors the ability to say so much in a few words. I might be struck by one line, and, always having a notebook nearby, I jot it down. These few moments establish a mindset for everything I do from that moment forward. What poets and prayers can say with such brevity feels powerful. Then, with the kick-start of caffeine, I'm ready to open the Bible and see what God might have for me there on a particular day. I'm better able to recognize scripture as a literary gift because I have set my mind on lyrical phrases before I begin.

On the days I have to leave early, and don't have time to sit with words on a page, I play a downloaded app in my car. The one I typically use opens with a musical interlude, followed by the reading of a scripture passage using ancient methods such as *lectio divina* (literally "divine reading"). In *lectio divina*, a short passage of scripture is read more than once, and the listener prayerfully considers the verses, listening for the words or phrases that seem to be locations of resonance. Out of that time come moments of reflection, meditation or contemplation, and finally prayer. A similar method to this is *visio divina* ("divine seeing"), where an individual focuses on a visual image, perhaps artwork, while praying.

I have friends who set a timer on their phones so they'll be reminded to pray during the day. I have added a formal prayer time at noon with nominal success, but have yet to accomplish seven times a day. When exploring these practices, we aren't giving ourselves a pass or fail grade. We're seeking God, and that looks different in our lives almost every day. It's relational, not mechanical.

My understanding of prayer has expanded to include all five senses as well. Individuals with sensory needs or conditions such as attention deficit hyperactivity disorder (ADHD) helped me understand the benefit of alerting your body to a time of stillness and prayer. Lighting a candle incorporates touch, sight, and smell in the praying process. Preparing a prayer corner in your home creates a sacred space that's used exclusively (to the extent possible) for a time of prayer. Sitting on your knees or lying facedown, one assumes a posture of prayer. Holding a prayer book, prayer beads, or an icon can be helpful in focusing one's attention on talking with God.

In the introduction to her book *Prayer in the Night: For Those Who Work, Who Watch, Who Weep*, Tish Harrison Warren opens with a tragic story of having a miscarriage. In the midst of being administered a blood transfusion, she demands her husband open his Book of Common Prayer and pray Compline, the liturgy prayed at the end of the day. The words had the desired calming effect and Warren joined her husband, praying the words she knew by heart.

It wasn't the formality she sought in these scary moments. In her words, "I needed this moment of crisis to find its place in something greater: the prayers of the church, yes, but more, the vast mystery of God, the surety of God's power, the reassurance of God's goodness."

I am new to the use of written prayers and the benefits of praying "by heart" continue to surprise me. The ability of these familiar words to draw someone into communion with the saints, across time and space, is a common occurrence, though. I've heard many stories like Warren's over the years. Prayers, creeds, and catechism responses remind Christians we are in this life together. Not only does Christ stick with us, we are bound together as the body of Christ as well.

I have a story of my own that parallels Warren's need to pray Compline. Our daughter was eight years old and she'd been playing at the neighbors, all weekend. It was the middle of summer, with no set schedule, and we kept getting texts of photos, showing what a grand time the girls were having. I figured if the neighbors had something they needed to do, they would send her home. I remember it being dinnertime, and I'd just put some ground beef on the stovetop to brown. My phone rang and my husband went to answer it.

"Your daughter's broken her arm," the neighbor said.

"Are you sure it's broken?" he asked. They talked for a few more seconds, while I hurriedly turned off the stove and put the hamburger skillet in the refrigerator.

We were on our way to the car when they pulled up with our little girl. The husband had her in his arms, and he choked out repeatedly, "I'm sorry. So sorry." She was limp, her face pale, except for her lips, which were a tinge of blue. Our girl was in shock.

On the drive to the emergency room, I sat in the back seat with her, stabilizing the arm as best I could. The bone protruded slightly, which is how the neighbor had known right away it was broken. My husband broke the law that day, speeding to the emergency room as fast as he could. In those moments, my knee-jerk reaction was to start praying in earnest, but I was seated in the car, so getting down on my knees was not an option. I found I didn't have a single extemporaneous prayer in me. My mind's entire focus was on the frail little girl lying on my lap, and being there for any need she might have. Watching for any way at all I could help her. "God, help" only took me so far. I started with the Jesus Prayer (Lord Jesus Christ, have mercy on me, a sinner), moving on to the Lord's Prayer. I prayed them quietly, almost under my breath, over my daughter, over the speeding vehicle, over the emergency room staff who didn't yet know we were coming. I moved on to the Apostles' Creed (I believe in God the Father Almighty . . .) but discovered I didn't have it memorized well enough to call up these belief statements. Does anyone even pray the creeds? So I rotated through the Jesus Prayer, the Lord's Prayer, and the words to "Amazing Grace." How's that for a trifecta? It worked. A familiar calm came over me. I found the strength I needed to make it through the car ride, get my daughter checked in, and receive the care she needed. It was a long and scary night, but I knew we were not alone.

Prayer is more about creating a habit than it is being good at it. When my daughter broke her arm, I could clearly see the benefit of having liturgical prayers memorized. They come automatically. Memory verses and hymns can come to us as well and turn into prayers. Praying was the thread I needed to connect me to the God who knit my daughter together in my womb (Psalm 139:13) and he would put her back together again. Formal prayers connected me to the greater body of Christ, even before I had a chance to ask anyone to pray. Once I got to the emergency room, I texted loved ones who I knew would pray for us. We carry one another's burdens in this way.

That long night in the hospital, and a few times since, I've felt tremors of anxiety. It's as if I'm staring in the face of a figurative monster I can't control. I have friends who deal with a more severe anxiety, a debilitating condition, on a regular basis. I've gotten the slightest sense of what this panic can cause, feeling as if the bottom might drop out when it hasn't yet and it might not, but you can't rationalize it away—truly shaky ground for many. In a discussion thread on Twitter, I asked people about the ways prayer (along with medication where appropriate) has helped them with anxiety. I'll share a few of their thoughts with you. Honesty is always a good place to start. God is big enough to hear your distress, face your anger, hold your fears. Pray your truth. Honest prayer may also allow us to step back and be reminded of what is real, beyond our spiraling emotions and thoughts. When you can't find the words, turn to the prayers of others—the psalms and books of prayer may give form to what is unformed in your pain. Place yourself in comforting scripture passages by inserting your name into God's assurances of presence. Long prayers are not required—pray short, staccato-type prayers like "help God" or "please Lord" out loud while taking deep breaths.

The last one in this list, praying and breathing, is one of the most effective prayers for the actual moment when the bottom drops out right before your eyes. Let's turn again to the ancient prayer called "breath prayer." Think of a simple phrase that can be said in one breath. There are two I regularly use. I vividly remember being in the car, listening to the radio the day of the Sandy Hook elementary school shooting in 2012. I quickly turned off the radio, and the first words out of my mouth were [inhale], "Lord, have mercy" [exhale]. It was the best prayer I knew to offer up for this community tragedy, asking God in his mercy to work in that horrific situation. Another prayer I commonly use, especially for those who receive devastating news, is [inhale], "Lord Jesus, draw near" [exhale].

Thinking through my own approach to prayer often leaves me wondering what to teach my daughter about prayer. We've always prayed the priestly blessing over her before bedtime each night: "The Lord bless you and keep you; the Lord make his face shine upon you, and be gracious to you; the Lord lift up his countenance upon you, and give you peace" (Numbers 6:24–26, NKJV). She's always excited when a pastor uses these familiar words as a closing benediction, and recently we've learned a song that includes this passage in the lyrics.

Other than that, we've mostly taught her prayer is a conversation with God. We pray for friends and family, not always together but we talk about praying for them. I did not grow up in a home that prayed before meals, so we don't do that with regularity, but on occasion. She has an Episcopal youth prayer book, *Call on Me: A Prayer Book for Young People*, a prayer rope from an Orthodox monastery, and she ends her day with prayer after reading from a devotional book. In time, I'm confident she'll respond well to learning other ways to pray. It's an area where we can continue to grow as a family.

Now, when I consider prayer, I'm not concerned about being good at it anymore. I think of it as a spiritual muscle, in need of regular exercise. If it doesn't seem possible to get up at four thirty in the morning and sit with your head bowed and eyes closed for an hour before starting the rest of your day, that doesn't mean you should write prayer off. Find new ways to pray. Incorporate tangible items in your prayer life. Start a journal to record the day's happenings or simply list those for whom you want to pray on a regular basis. Use the psalms as a prayer tool. Dance your prayers. Find a book of prayers. Walk or run your prayers. Paint or photograph your prayers. Write out your prayers. The limits we place on prayer come only from us. God is always willing and eager to communicate. Keep at it.

CHAPTER 9

An Interview That Had
Me Nervous

I had to leave childish things behind before I even had the chance to be childish.

—Marlena Graves, *A Beautiful Disaster*

H ere in this section on prayer, I want to share a story about my friend Kevin. He has given me permission to do so. I don't know if Kevin was taught to pray as a child, but if he was, it would appear many of his prayers went unanswered. Kevin went through a lot before meeting the only one who truly saves us. Jesus. In the process of defining the parameters of this book, when we decided to address those times when the bottom drops out, this conversation with Kevin came to mind right away. It points to the beautiful truth, God does answer our prayers, although we don't always fully understand how, and sometimes it takes a while.

Since releasing my first book, I've done interviews for podcasts and YouTube channels. One conversation I had was with a friend from Twitter. While Kevin and I hadn't interacted too much, when he asked for an interview, I said yes. We scheduled a date, and, as I try to do before all my podcast interviews, I visited his website and listened to a previous episode.

Kevin's story broke my heart. As he would tell you, he doesn't share the details for sympathy, but it's full of tragedy and misfortune. Kevin's growing-up years were not like mine. Mine weren't perfect, but they felt relatively secure. I had two parents who lived in the same house and raised my brothers and me. I knew who my family was and emerged from childhood with an overall sense of innocence. Kevin was not given this privilege.

Often when I give interviews, I share church stories. We're honest about the imperfections of the church, but the conversations quickly turn to a Bible story or a visit I've made to a church service different from my own or a spiritual practice I've recently discovered. It's familiar territory.

I could see immediately that my conversation with Kevin would not be as easy. Any kind of lighthearted conversation would be inauthentic. I didn't know exactly what we'd cover in our interview, but you can't know the details of Kevin's life, as they're revealed in his YouTube recordings, and talk about happy-clappy church. No way.

Considering all this, a question entered my mind. Especially in circumstances like Kevin's—a life of adoption, foster families, homelessness, sexual abuse as a child, drugs and alcohol—this question demanded answers.

The question: Is the gospel good news for everyone? I couldn't get it out of my head. I asked about it on a social media outlet. I had an answer for myself, but sometimes what we know by faith to be true can be hard to express in words. Honestly, I grew quite nervous about having this conversation at all.

The day of the interview came and I set up my "office" outdoors on the back patio. Weather permitting, I always give interviews out there because, living in a rural area, outdoors offers the most consistent, reliable internet. Going back to listen to the interview now, Kevin starts by observing the beautiful location and the sound of birds and my wind chime.

The conversation quickly takes a turn. I admit to him I was nervous about the interview. He admitted being nervous, but for different reasons than mine. To him, I seem so put together. I know how to talk church and scripture. From my perspective, I kept thinking, where was Jesus when you were treated so badly? When you felt so incredibly lonely and lost, and hopeless?

I'd read books on these kinds of questions we all ask ourselves at one point or another. Rabbi Harold Kushner's *When Bad Things Happen to Good People* and *When God Doesn't Make Sense* by James C. Dobson. During Lent last year, I read *Everything Happens for a Reason: And Other Lies I've Loved* by Kate Bowler. Here's what she writes about the initial days following her diagnosis with stage IV colon cancer: "At a time when I should have felt abandoned by God, I was not reduced to ashes. I felt like I was floating, floating on the love and prayers of all those who hummed around me like worker bees. . . . They came in like priests and mirrored back to me the face of Jesus."

But this wasn't some late-night conversation talking theology with a friend. Sitting before me—on Zoom—was a real person who had likely struggled with this question in a highly personal way. With tears in my eyes, I said this:

> Kevin, what happened to you was truly horrific and the hurdles that you have overcome, the hours of therapy I would imagine you have spent . . . but what I was nervous about; we don't have answers for what happened in your life. We don't have answers for bad things that have happened in my life, or anyone's. Sometimes we get glimpses, but by and large, we don't always. God is God, you know, he wants us to know the parts of himself that he has made known, and those are beautiful and they carry us through and they give me a tremendous amount of hope, and that's what I like to give to others if I can, on his behalf.

Kevin had his own reasons for being nervous. "This is why I was very nervous about talking to you today [clears throat]; nothing has to be perfect except his love for us. There's nothing else I'm looking for that, um, is going to replace that, is going to lift me up and keep me up, right? Nothing else but my understanding of his love for me."

Jesus the healer. Kevin needs him. I need him. We all do.

Kevin went on to say, "There's hope that out of all this pain and suffering and tragedy, and mourning, and I've had to mourn greatly for everything I've lost; there's redemption—would be fair—there's, um, there's a resurrection and that is really, that would have been unfathomable to me to even consider that."

My mind settled on the two *re-* words he used. Some of my favorite Christian talk. Re-demption and re-surrection, or *re-surgere* in Latin, "to rise." Yes, we have to do the work. There should be a grieving for what has happened. There's often a need for professional help in walking through the pain. It takes a certain amount of time, and we don't control the time frame. There are conversations to be had, and some of them will be hard. But when we invite Jesus to be a part of the process, when we ask him to do the work in us and with us, and in our life situations, there is redemption. We walk *through* it. We emerge a new creature, not entirely unbeaten, but healing. Resurrected, as one who comes up from the ashes and dares to ask God to make our lives things of glory.

In preparing for the interview, I gave some thought to a Bible character who could help us better understand what Kevin had gone through. Job came to mind. When the book of Job starts out, readers are told he has it all. God even brags on Job to Satan. "Have you considered my servant Job? There is no one like him on the earth, a blameless and upright man who fears God and turns away from evil" (Job 1:8).

From this initial conversation, Job's story responds to this same timeless question, Why do bad things happen to good people? God allows Satan to wreak havoc in Job's life. He loses his children, livestock, property. Then his health deteriorates. What remains, his wife and friends, don't appear to be much in the way of consolation prizes. Job's world gets shaken up like a snow globe, and then someone comes along and throws the globe against a concrete wall.

After these cruel things happen to Job, we read some accusations from his wife, some pretty bad advice from friends, some serious lamenting from Job, and finally a closing word from God.

This book is not about easy answers. As I told Kevin in our conversation, "God is God."

Job's parting words have captivated me over the years. Every time I read them, I get chills. I knew, especially after getting to know him a little more, Kevin could relate. "I had heard of you by the hearing of the ear, but now my eye sees you" (Job 42:5).

The question becomes, then, how do we walk alongside one another when we can't fix it? When there are no easy answers? When we feel nervous about knowing what we know, but want to be at the very least a kind human, and more, a vessel of the hope Jesus offers? As I told Kevin,

> We never want to appear insensitive and sometimes I feel like Christian people, those representing Jesus, can try to give easy answers, and I didn't, I don't in any way want to negate what happened to you. All I know is that my faith has taught me whether it's something I'm going through, or the things you've gone through, we could both list a ton of people, Jesus just makes that better, um, his presence is healing.

Suppress the desire to offer answers. Don't walk away. Use the kindest words you know, which may include a scripture or two, but maybe not. Pray with them if they ask you to do so. Bring the individuals to Jesus on your own too, through prayer, through your presence. He is the only one who truly heals.

CHAPTER 10

The Original Prayer Book

My God in his steadfast love will meet me; my God will let
me look in triumph on my enemies.

—David, Psalm 59:10

N o matter what you're feeling, there's a psalm for that.
The psalms are prayers and songs used in Jewish worship.
They form the backbone of Christian hymns, prayer books,
spirituals, and any number of worship songs. Realizing these lyrical
lines have meanings that transcend time and place adds to their significance. One primary way I read scripture includes learning more
about the historical context. Often the disconnect between a book of
the Bible and the individual reader is knowledge about the intent of
the book or passage. However, in considering the psalms as prayer
and song, we don't want to look for "only the facts"—any quick Google search would provide us with that. I reached a place spiritually
where I wanted to know their function as a spiritual discipline. Like
many other portions of scripture, I wanted to know the psalms to my
core. Since scripture is inspired by God (2 Timothy 3:16), I wanted
the melody of my heart to be the songs of God's people. How could
all the talk of enemies (did I even have any?) and emotion and judgment of people and nations have meaning in my personal life?

The psalms grew in significance for me when I began reading the Bible chronologically. It helped to place the psalms within
the Old Testament stories. For example, some of David's psalms
were written when he was on the run from King Saul. Note the

beginning of Psalm 57, when David fled from Saul into a cave. It gives heightened meaning to the opening verse: "Be merciful to me, O God, be merciful to me, for in you my soul takes refuge; in the shadow of your wings I will take refuge, until the destroying storms pass by" (Psalm 57:1).

In his book *Open and Unafraid: The Psalms as a Guide to Life,* W. David O. Taylor writes, "There is no such thing as a modern individualist in the psalms. It is a fundamentally communal book where individuals find their place in the world of faithfulness and faithlessness within the context of the community." Much like our other spiritual activities, even if we read the psalms to give voice to our personal emotions, to ground us in their truth, we carry this healthier spirituality into our interactions with others. Maybe we're not going through a particular trial, but we hear of someone who is, and we're reading the psalms, and the person's name comes to mind. Suddenly, we find ourselves praying on behalf of this person, because the words speak directly to their situation. I often reach out to the person when this happens. Their response is usually something along these lines: "It helps to know I'm not alone."

I remember reading Psalm 73 some time back, and I'm sure I had read it before, but it hit at a right time in my life, and it caught my attention because I felt as if I could have written it. For weeks, I read that psalm, praying God would see my heart for his people. In the psalm, Asaph, a chief musician during the reign of David, acknowledges God is good to the pure in heart but admits there are times it appears the arrogant and wicked are the ones who are flourishing. They seem to be walking on easy street, and they boast about it, and the people praise them. When Asaph thinks back on all the religious practices he follows to keep his heart clean and maintain innocence, it doesn't seem to matter. My favorite verse is the turning point of the psalm. "If I had said, 'I will talk on in this way,' I would have been untrue to the circle of your children" (Psalm 73:15). At this point, Asaph goes into God's sanctuary. It is there, in the presence of God, he's reminded of the fate the arrogant and wicked have waiting for them. He breaks out into praise to God, who is the strength of his heart.

As I prayed over this psalm on a regular basis, I asked God to help me stop comparing myself to others. If I started feeling like things were unfair, focusing on it to the point of being fixated, I asked God for discernment about what things I should say aloud—on social media, in my writing, at my church, over coffee with friends—and what things to bring to him alone. There's a fine line between sharing our thoughts in an effort to make things better, and airing dirty laundry, as they say. This idea of bringing my thoughts to God first, asking him how I can best glorify him, has become a general practice in my life. When I pray this psalm, and visualize Asaph entering God's sanctuary, I remember in whom I've placed my trust, "my portion forever" (Psalm 73:26). This process restores my hope.

The idea of incorporating a regular rhythm of psalm-reading is not new. People have been doing this since Old Testament times. As a first-century Jewish man, Jesus would have known the psalms and often quoted them. Shortly after the fall of the Roman Empire (476 CE), a man named Benedict grew disgruntled with the paganism he found in Rome and retreated to the wilderness outside of the city. Eventually, other men wanting to pursue the religious life convinced him to form a monastic community. He wrote a booklet referred to simply as *The Rule*, which includes a specific schedule of praying through the psalms so that these monks sang their way through the book of psalms in a week. That's ambitious.

In *Cloister Walk*, Kathleen Norris writes about her experience spending extended periods of time with Benedictine monks at St. John's Abbey in Minnesota. She notes the Benedictine method has lengthy moments of silence between each psalm. "As a poet I like to be with words. It was a revelation to me that this could be prayer; that this could be enough." Prayer without words. Prayer between the words. I've known this kind of prayer when my daughter is hurting and I don't know how or if I should try to help. When I lift her up in prayer, sometimes I don't even know what to ask God for in her life. Sitting with her, those times she's facing what can only be called "growing-up moments," the prayers between the words have to be enough.

This made me wonder how these lengthy moments of silence benefit the monks who are reading the psalms. When we hear the emotionally charged words of a psalm, we need a minute to catch up spiritually. Maybe to offer praise or acknowledge sorrow or express anger. We shouldn't rush past the relational aspect of the psalms. There's you, and God, and the author, and the people around you. Imagine the monastery Norris writes about in her book. These men live with one another 24/7. In those moments of silence, between the psalms, they're allowing the spirit to work among them. Maybe this is the only way they could live together for years and not run away screaming.

And can we scream at God? Can we be honest about what we deem unfair, or just plain wrong? What if we're raging mad over an injustice that's happened to us or we're angered on behalf of someone else? As a little girl, I memorized Psalm 139:23: "Search me, O God, and know my heart; test me and know my thoughts," as a stand-alone verse. Considering the context, specifically the two verses preceding it, it's a powerful prayer, where David is acknowledging hatred, and asking God to line his heart up with God's ways. "Do I not hate those who hate you, O Lord? And do I not loathe those who rise up against you? I hate them with perfect hatred; I count them my enemies" (Psalm 139:21–22). As a child, I don't know if I would have comprehended the full picture of what these verses teach us about bringing strong emotions to God, but it's a comfort to me now, knowing we can.

Taking our rage to God is the safest space for us to express it. As the proverb teaches us: "Trust in the Lord with all your heart, and do not rely on your own insight; in all your ways acknowledge him, and he will make straight your paths" (Proverbs 3:5–6). Notice the action steps required here. Trust in the Lord. Don't rely on your own insight. Acknowledge him. God's action step is to make straight your paths. Trusting him means knowing we can be our truest self before him. We bring God our emotions, we acknowledge he sees our whole self, and he invites us to walk with him on the straight (other translations say right) paths. Ask God to help you trust him, to show you where you need to acknowledge (submit to or surrender to) him, and to make your paths straight— even if your legs are still shaking as you walk down that path. The emotions might remain too, but you can trust God is guiding your steps. David's psalms and Solomon's proverb point to a desire to include God in every aspect of one's life.

As I learned about people incorporating a regular reading of the psalms in their daily life, I decided to try reading a psalm a day for a month. I'd picked up a copy of the Common English Bible and not used it yet, so I turned to the middle of that Bible for this project. It's a more recent translation written in a conversational style, which seemed ideal for incorporating the psalms into my daily prayer time. The psalms gave me words of praise to echo back to God, along with honest thoughts about how the wicked seem to flourish. Most of the time, the psalmist and I came back around to praising God. Making this a regular daily practice would certainly affect our thinking habits. I did not make it a whole month, and I missed a few days in the week or so I did read a psalm. Although I wasn't successful, if we're defining success as marking off a daily to-do list, I can always try again. There's an abundance of grace in our spiritual disciplines, and we can know God will use whatever efforts we do put forth.

There's another method of praying the psalms I have done with regularity. I was gifted the Coptic Orthodox prayer book, the *Agpia*. It is organized in sections, based on the hours an individual might pray. There's also an introduction that starts off every time of prayer.

The introductory prayer always begins with "In the name of the Father, and the Son, and the Holy Spirit, one God. Amen." I read it aloud the first few mornings, and with barely a thought, my hands joined in the effort, making the sign of the cross. As I settled into reading these words, my breath came along; in and out.

Each hour of prayer also includes the Lord's Prayer. I had read about a Jewish practice of praying the Shema with the palm of the hand covering their eyes to block out distraction. I hoped they wouldn't mind if I borrowed the gesture as I prayed the words of Christ. Having this prayer memorized, I could do it with my eyes closed, literally.

The introductory prayer section of the *Agpia* concludes with Psalm 51, before the unique scripture passages and prayers for a specific hour begin. This means you would potentially pray Psalm 51 seven times a day if you used the whole book—this practice requires some serious discipline. When you pray passages of scripture like this every day, the words wash over you. I've yet to memorize them, but I know the work they do in my spirit. I've experienced how they soften my heart toward others. Praying regularly like this stills my mind, and that's an accomplishment all in itself. At varying times, different words or phrases jump off the page. The following phrases are from the New King James Version:

"According to Your lovingkindness,"

If God has offered such loving-kindness to me, what should my response be? Who in my circle could use a little more loving-kindness from me? How would my life look different if my actions poured out from the realization that God shows me loving-kindness?

"According to the multitude of Your tender mercies,"

What would make mercy tender? David penned (chiseled?) this passage after being called out for his adulterous act with Bathsheba. Knowing this, if I put myself in his shoes (sandals): knowing God's mercy is still there for me and knowing how desperately I need it in that moment, of course it is tender.

"Against You, You only, have I sinned,"

Every sin. They are carried out against God because they put distance between me and my creator. What might feed my pride, what might be acceptable in the eyes of others, if done from a wrong intention in my heart, is sin against my God. This makes me more conscientious about sinning, and repenting.

"Purge me with hyssop, and I shall be clean."

I remember doing a word search on "purge" in the original Hebrew, "to remove by cleansing" or "de-sin." The hyssop branch is full of symbolic references. Soldiers offered Jesus a sponge dripping with sour wine, extended on a hyssop branch (John 19:28–30). When I prayed these words day after day, I could focus on them in a new way, calling to mind other places in scripture that a particular word or phrase was used. It further wove the Bible into one amazing, interconnected story.

We interact with God differently based on what we're going through in life. The psalms teach us this. Whether as an individual or in community, we can bring all our emotions to God. Sometimes everything is coming up praises, and words like this are a good fit: "You are my God, and I will give thanks to you; you are my God, I will extol you. O give thanks to the Lord, for he is good, for his steadfast love endures forever" (Psalm 118:28–29).

Other times we might be filled with sorrow, or weary from everything that's going on in life. We still trust that God is with us, and what we offer might sound something more like this: "I cry to you, O Lord; I say, 'You are my refuge, my portion in the land of the living.' Give heed to my cry, for I am brought very low" (Psalm 142:5–6).

Like many of you, I grow frustrated with the Church for poorly representing Christ, mostly because I see our divine potential, and love the Church too much to not hold us accountable. Our quarrels and divisions, the lack of charity we show the marginalized, and the numerous abuses reported, with little to no compassion for the victims. What happens within our church walls too often mirrors the discord and abuse we see in the world around us, and this should not be so. For those who have written off church or have watched our seemingly hypocritical acts from a distance without ever joining in, their hearts break along with ours at reprehensible things in this world like sex trafficking, acts of racism, displaced refugees, civil and political unrest. For these wrongs, we can turn to the psalms of lament because we can, and we should, talk to God this way: "O God, you have rejected us, broken our defenses; you have been angry; now restore us! You have caused the land to quake; you have torn it open; repair the cracks in it, for it is tottering. You have made your people suffer hard things; you have given us wine to drink that made us reel" (Psalms 60:1–3).

I read a social media post that wondered at the fact that evangelical churches, who place such a high emphasis on the importance of scripture, don't read the psalms in our worship services. There's a great deal of value in praying these psalms of praise, fear, weariness, and communal lament together. Sharing a psalm that expresses a person's fear helps us remember fear is a natural human response. It reminds us that although we might not be experiencing a certain emotion, say sorrow, right now, there are those around us who are. We see it on their faces. We may know of circumstances firsthand. Sometimes the psalms will say exactly what you're going through, and you'll wonder how, right then, you could happen to come across those specific words you needed to hear. You're glad you don't have to carry the burdens of life alone. We share these human moments and it builds empathy in us. We're able to step outside of our individual existence and realize we are in this together. The psalmists felt things as we do, those hearing or praying the psalms around you feel all these things too. How much better off would we be if we turned to the psalms, and other readings in scripture, to express what we're going through as a local church, but further, as a collective body of believers? Think of how our congregations could benefit from praying the psalms, becoming familiar with the different expressions we find in them, so when congregants are on their own, they'll know where to turn.

Imagine if, as a body of believers, we cried out together, "I lift up my eyes to the hills—from where will my help come? My help comes from the Lord, who made heaven and earth" (Psalm 121:1–2). Go ahead and make the verses plural. I often do, and this helps me recall I don't ever pray the psalms alone.

CHAPTER 11

A Reflection on Habakkuk

The oracle that the prophet Habakkuk saw. O LORD, how long shall I cry for help, and you will not listen? Or cry to you "Violence!" and you will not save? Why do you make me see wrongdoing and look at trouble? Destruction and violence are before me; strife and contention arise. So the law becomes slack and justice never prevails. The wicked surround the righteous—therefore judgment comes forth perverted.

—Habakkuk 1:1–4

We've learned more about the psalms, and the permission they give us to talk to God with utter honesty. As I've studied the prophets, I see similar communication. In the case of the books of prophets we find toward the end of the Old Testament, whether it's the prophets speaking on God's behalf or a community registering their complaint with God, these books are raw emotion. God often sent prophets to the people of God and the surrounding nations, warning about things to come, and always reminding them no matter what trouble his people might go through, God still loved them with an everlasting love. Habakkuk, though, reads a little differently. Instead of telling the people what God had to say, he speaks to God on behalf of the people.

A Job-like figure, Habakkuk has a conversation with God. In two short chapters, he dialogues with God, and the final chapter concludes with a psalm. Like Job, we don't know much about

Habakkuk's birthplace or lineage, though his literary style suggests he was well educated.

In Habakkuk's day, the Northern Kingdom has already fallen to the Assyrians, and Judah seems to be weakening as well, eventually falling to the Babylonians. Both of these nations were known for their tyrannical rule. To make matters worse, Habakkuk sees before him a corrupt Jewish government. Shaky times. God had given his people the Promised Land, but might he also take it away from them?

So Habakkuk has a conversation with God about all this. For two chapters, they go back and forth. It becomes a classic case of, "Can I say that to God?" Habakkuk doesn't hold back. God responds, not giving a full explanation of what is going on in the world Habakkuk is lamenting, but clarifying a few things. God reveals plans for the Chaldeans (Babylonians), who would take over the Southern Kingdom and then eventually fall themselves. Habakkuk cannot believe what God tells him. Unlike another biblical prophet, Jonah, Habakkuk doesn't run as God reveals part of his plan. No time in the belly of a big fish for him. He stands before God and responds, "Your eyes are too pure to behold evil, and you cannot look on wrongdoing; why do you look on the treacherous, and are silent when the wicked swallow those more righteous than they?" (Habakkuk 1:13).

Yes, you can. You can talk to God that way.

God gives Habakkuk more insight. He reveals five woes that will come right on time. Our God does not miss a thing. "But the Lord is in his holy temple; let all the earth keep silence before him!" (Habakkuk 2:20).

What follows in chapter three is a psalm. Like other psalms, it first acknowledges God as sovereign, moving into lament, then into remembrance, and ending in praise. Notations in 3:1 and at the end in 3:19 indicate it became a confession the people would use in communal worship. Taken from Eugene Peterson's *The Message*: "God, I've heard what our ancestors say about you, and I'm stopped in my tracks, down on my knees. Do among us what you did among them. Work among us as you worked among them. And as you bring judgment, as you surely must, remember mercy" (Habakkuk 3:2).

■ ■ ■

Method: Habakkuk is one of the twelve minor prophets, so we know his book isn't long (more on this in the following paragraph). Making note of this, I looked up the time period when he prophesied, and who his contemporaries were, including kings and prophets. I researched the following: Northern Kingdom or Southern Kingdom; preexile, exile, or postexile; and noted his literary style. All of this helps a reader better understand the message prophets had for people of their day, for a future biblical time, or into the end times.

One more tidbit about Habakkuk: I learned the books of the Bible in order, but also by category. In the Old Testament, there is the law, history, poetry, major prophets, and minor prophets. It's always bothered me that we labeled some prophet books as minor, when their messages were anything but that. They're labeled as such because of the size of each book, compared to the lengthier, major prophets. I mentioned this on Twitter and received a much-appreciated correction. Many scholars call these twelve books of prophecy The Twelve. They are found on one scroll in ancient manuscripts. From now on, I'm calling the minor prophets the Twelve, and I have written it in my bible index as such.

Would you pray with me?

God, we're still here. Things around us seem shaky, and life has us weary. In the midst of the turmoil, we choose as Habakkuk did to rejoice in you, the giver of salvation and our strength. Amen.

CHAPTER 12

A Lament over Division

A lament is an appeal to God based on confidence in His character.

—Glenn Packiam, N. T. Wright online

One spiritual practice has a book of the Bible named after it—lament is Lamentations. If I asked what it meant to lament, the answers would be all over the place. If I asked you what the book of Lamentations is about, similar results. We don't discuss lament very often because it makes us feel uncomfortable. We're not even sure we're supposed to lament, bringing our raw emotions to God. It's not how many of us were raised. We might even think anger is a sin. Most of us, though, face disillusionment of one sort or another: things not going as we dreamed they would back in the days of our beautiful, innocent beginnings, and we may find ourselves angry or sorrowful about this new reality. When that's the case, lament is a way to talk with God about it. Think about a time you faced a difficulty in life, and it left you in despair. Just thinking about it now might bring up strong emotions. Lament gives you an outlet, helping you prayerfully process the situation. Dare to ask God to show you gifts, big or small, even in that particular circumstance. Remember, we can talk to God that way.

When we see injustice in the world, like Habakkuk we can direct our words of lament to God, giving our angst a voice. The practice of lament can include praying passages from the psalms or elsewhere in scripture, writing one in your own words, or reading a lament someone else has written. Whether we lament individually or with others, we'll soon see it ends up being a communal action. We're reminded we are a people who live in the tension of the now and not yet. Our times of struggle can eventually grow our compassion for others. We rely on things like grace and mercy a little more, and we see the reality of things more clearly. I have found the process of lament softens my touch as I extend a hand to others. Most of all, for me, I need reminding that ours is a God who sees. A God of love, and justice.

Beyond those moments of liturgical significance like Ash Wednesday or the season of Lent (for those churches who observe the liturgical calendar), lament is not something the modern church focuses on. It's a practice that could be of great benefit as we reflect on the unsteady and conflicted world we find ourselves in, and take responsibility for our part in the fallen nature of things.

As one for whom the Church—the full, whole, abundantly loved body of Christ—is so important, I am especially grieved over the ways we dismiss and deny other beloved children of God. There is much in the world to lament; this is one that I carry, knowing that each of us will have our own set of lamentations. And as we carry each other's burdens, I offer the following lament over the ways I see the Church falling short of our intended purpose, hoping you will join my prayer:

O God,

  We are broken. Truly, the bottom would drop out altogether if not for your sustaining hand. We harm our children, damaging the world around them, and robbing them of their innocence. We neglect those you called us to care for; the foreigners, the orphans, and the widows. Online, using a tool meant to connect us, we hurl insults and say things to one another we would never say face-to-face. It makes this world feel like an angry, cold place. It seems we are more separated economically, politically, and socially every day. How desperately we need your light to illuminate the darkness.

Look at the wreckage we have made of your body on this earth. The body of Christ is called to be salt, a desirable flavor, light, a bright and warming presence, and a city on a hill, a destination travelers want to experience. We know the way, the truth, the life, and we don't tell those hurting beside us, all around us. In our unity, may others believe you sent me—that was Christ's final prayer.

Lord, Lord, where is our unity? We draw lines in the sand, deciding for ourselves who is in and who is out. As if it is our gospel to distribute as we deem fit. We throw stones at the marginalized; women, singles, children, homosexuals, and those forced to abandon their homes. Father, remind us afresh, these three remain: faith, hope, and love, but the greatest of these is love (1 Corinthians 13:13).

Our dividing lines are poor indicators of our love for you and for one another. We don't celebrate our differences, trusting you to bring us all together in Jesus's name. We do not learn from one another, but cluster in groups that look just like us. For the times I think I might not be part of the problem, remind me I am but one member of the body of Christ. As the body moves, so go its individual parts. Lord, open our eyes that we might better see one another.

We remember the nations you brought together at Pentecost (Acts 2:9–11); the Parthians, Medes, Elamites; residents of Mesopotamia, Judea and Cappadocia, Pontus and Asia, Phrygia and Pamphylia, Egypt and the parts of Libya near Cyrene; visitors from Rome (both Jews and converts to Judaism); Cretans and Arabs. Believers from all these nations and cultures, joined together under the headship of Christ, receiving the great gift of the Holy Spirit.

Spirit, do it again. Help us set aside the labels we use to separate us from one another and form us into one body of believers—one body. May we love one another, may our shoes be readied with the gospel of peace (Ephesians 6:15), as we join you in the eternal work of making things right again.

In the name of the Father, the Son, and the Holy Spirit. Amen.

PART III

ANCHORED

CHAPTER 13

Opening Up the Bible

A Bible that's falling apart usually belongs to someone who isn't.

—Charles Spurgeon

Bible study rescued me. I don't say this flippantly. During those years when we were trying to sell a house and looking for a new home, Bible study gave me a focus. I was very pregnant the September I joined a study group at the church we attend now, and over the years, the women in Bible study have embraced both my daughter and me. They have shown my daughter how to walk in almost every stage of life imaginable and remain faithful to God. I have asked these women to pray for circumstances over the years and basked in the assurance of knowing they do. They have listened sympathetically to my disappointments and celebrated with me when the news was good. It has helped me to carry their burdens and share in their times of happiness too. I realized how much good it did me to serve others when my natural inclination would have been to focus on my own problems. We can get so caught up in our own joys and concerns; being part of a group where offering support was as important as receiving support helped me to look beyond my individual circumstances. We all crave a place where it's safe to be our whole selves. Friendship, especially brought together in Christ as sisterhood, is next level.

Over the years, the women in attendance at Bible study have changed, but the Spirit who brings us together has not. The mix of ages, stages in life, mature and less mature Christians, has helped us take a look at our individual faiths. In our everyday lives, what we've walked through together forms an exhausting list. Health scares, job loss, infidelity, children who seem to have walked away from their faith, death of spouses and parents, and a beloved Bible study teacher.

There have been women who stopped coming to Bible study suddenly. Often it was because they faced a crisis in their lives, and we all handle those challenging times differently. They couldn't face our group and share this hard news. Would they be judged? Did they have the strength to tell their whole story all over again to us? Where was God when it hurt like this? Others ran to us, needing the collective faith of the group to carry them. I hope we've ministered to both in their time of need.

I wish I could share with you here a foolproof, guided plan on how to have a successful Bible study or small group. So many of us long for this kind of connection. If I could prescribe the perfect group Bible study formula, we could cure loneliness. I've been a part of groups that didn't click for whatever reason. I've attended churches for months, years, and still felt like only a handful of people even knew my name. I do know this—for the last decade Bible study has been a lifeline for me. It hasn't been about the particular studies, some have been excellent and others *meh*, and it's not about the small group of us who have always been in attendance for all those years. What we've been able to develop is a group of women whose hearts are open to one another, and the Holy Spirit has illuminated the words of scripture in our midst. These studies kept telling us how much God loved us, and how Christ showed the deepest respect for women and others on the margins of society. Together, we embraced that worthiness we longed for, that Christ offered. We dared to take him at his word. It saddens me to hear people give the excuse of not knowing enough about the Bible to feel comfortable in Bible study. I've heard this from some people I've known. What better place to learn? Focus on being among people who long to grow in the faith like you do, and don't let anyone tell you that you don't belong there.

Jesus said, "For where two or three are gathered in my name, I am there among them" (Matthew 18:20). Does it have to be a formal Bible study? No. As with every other spiritual practice, pray to seek out what might work for you. Maybe it's a group of people in your neighborhood, a house church, a dinner club, two people getting together for coffee. If you've tried this a number of times before and it's been less than fulfilling, ask God to help you try again, one more time. If the experience felt damaging to you as a person or to your faith, there may be some intermediate steps toward healing to take first. When you sense God telling you the time is right, boldly ask him to send someone into your life who will extend an invitation. We've all participated in gatherings that haven't worked for whatever reason. I'm just here to tell you, when you find what works for you, it's life-giving.

■ ■ ■

One of the women in my study group introduced me to an entirely new way of reading scripture. She had picked up a chronological Bible and was using it for her daily reader. She kept mentioning insights she was discovering. When I saw a paperback version at a garage sale, I grabbed it and we decided to read it together beginning the following January. Eight years later, we're in a private Facebook group that reads through the Bible this way every year. I regularly see other groups doing this as well, including a Catholic contingency led by Father Mike Schmidt. I tend to buck all things trendy, but I am here for this one. Reading the Bible in the order scholars have best determined the events happened has been a life-changing way for me. I knew the Bible in bits and chunks. I had lists of verses to make my case about whatever point I was trying to make. Carrying memorized verses with me from childhood, I had God's word "hid in mine heart, that I might not sin against thee" (Psalm 119:11, KJV). I had studied the Bible by topic and by book. Now, I was reading it as God's story.

All those years I had listened to sermons and wondered how a pastor could have particular verses and passages at the ready when they were preaching. What would it take to have that kind of familiarity with scripture? Did it only come with a Bible degree? Now I know the hours one can put in each and every day. I know what it's like to soak in those truths. Quick recall will not happen overnight, but God honors our efforts. I also know what it's like to read a passage and offer it up to God, because it's a difficult one and at first glance, what those verses seem to say about God doesn't settle easily. I know the songs of God's people begin in Genesis, and we read them clear through to Revelation.

Please don't take this as a promotional blurb for one way I've found to read the Bible. Here's what I want you to take away: there are a number of ways to know God. We can learn of God in the natural world, in history, in church tradition, and from one another. But making time daily to read the Bible is a key component to learning how to follow Jesus. Much like prayer, and creating moments of silence, and all the other spiritual habits we're considering here, there is not one right way to spend time in God's word. I don't approach this as a short devotional read, a verse or two followed by an application question, check these off the list and you're good to go. No time in God's word is wasted, but if this is the only way we ever read the Bible, we'll never plumb its depths. As Esau McCauley put it in his excellent book *Reading While Black*, "For those of us who want to continue to affirm the ongoing normative role of the Bible in the life of the church, it will not do to dismiss the concerns raised about the Bible from many quarters. The path forward is not a return to the naïveté of a previous generation, but a journeying through the hard questions while being informed by the roots of the tradition bequeathed to us. I propose instead that we adopt the posture of Jacob and refuse to let go of the text until it blesses us."

I believe scripture is vital to our growth as a Christian and feel the need to pause here for a brief moment. My prayer for each of you is that you find a method of engagement with scripture that feeds you spiritually, and start there. Over time, add new methods and grow not only in biblical knowledge, but grow more in love with the time spent with God as you read the Bible. There is no reason for Bible reading to feel like a chore or a legalistic requirement hanging over our head.

That being said, for some of you, it's not about growth, but about an undoing. Scripture has been used as a legalistic weapon in your past, the words taken out of context and out of touch with a loving God who is forever drawing us to him. Your Bible-reading journey needs to happen in your own time and at your own pace. Maybe the idea of sitting down to read a whole book or passage at a time makes you cringe. But here you are, still reading as I go on about the fulfillment it has brought me. God walks this part of your journey with you too. Might I suggest you look up a verse online, by topic or from a certain book of the Bible you remember speaking to you in the past. Write that verse down on a notecard and keep it with you. Put it on the dashboard of your car or tuck it into your wallet. Place it on your nightstand or refrigerator. Let the words settle over you. Pray you'd be ready for another word from God, and another. If you stumble across a verse that triggers bad memories, sit with God in that. Ask God to reveal himself to you in that verse, and help you forget how someone else used it incorrectly. The Bible has the ability to shape our lives, but we might have to unlearn, then relearn certain parts in order to go further in our reading time. This too is wrestling.

The idea of wrestling with scripture, not looking for right answers but looking for God, is a common way of engaging with scripture. In Judaism, the Talmud is a collection of ancient rabbinic writings, and conversations, about the law, biblical interpretation, cultural understanding, and history. Much of this material is recorded from oral Jewish traditions. It links the understandings of Hebrew scripture, orthodoxy, with Jewish practices, orthopraxy. These complex layers of interaction included in the study of the written and oral laws are part of how the Jewish community has sought to understand and live out scripture over the years. There's a popular quote by Rebbetzin Dena Weinberg, founder and dean of EYAHT College of Jewish Studies for Women, "Torah is not education; it's transformation." Studying ancient Judaism has helped me in understanding scripture as a whole and learning how to read it as a transforming practice.

Of all the spiritual disciplines I've practiced, reading the Bible chronologically, an average of three or four chapters a day, has perhaps made the greatest impact. Much like the church calendar offers a year-round rhythm to our days, I'm establishing a scripture rhythm in my life as well. In fifteen or twenty minutes, I cannot study a passage in its entirety, or spend too much time contemplating a scene I'm reading. Reading the Bible through like this is more about grasping the big picture. It has forced me to read passages I would otherwise skip over (think long lists of names and temple measurements), realizing they have things to teach us about God as well. It might be similar to those who have a practice of reading the Bible through a church lectionary, lists of scripture passages that include a set of readings from the Old Testament, a psalm, one of the four gospels, and an epistle or something else from the New Testament. My year starts out in Genesis, of course, and January goes by in a blur. How can one book include so much detail? Jesus comes on the biblical scene on September 25. On my birthday, I turn to Luke every year, and he tells me about the many women who supported Jesus's earthly ministry. A large part of December, the season of Advent, is spent reading 2 Peter, Jude, and Revelation, declaring that Christ is coming back again. The liturgical season and these books of the Bible fit well together.

As a parent, I've had to think through what I wanted to teach our daughter about the importance of God's word in her life. As a little girl, she had children's Bibles, but I got her a "big girl" Bible before she could even read it. I wanted her to see and hold the Bible in its fullness to develop a sense for the lifelong pursuit of using it to better know God. With her dad and me, she read through *The Action Bible* chronologically at an early age, maybe eight or nine? She's reading *The Message* Bible from cover to cover now. Perhaps most importantly, she's always seen me reading my Bible. From an early age, she knew not to interrupt Mom too much when I sat down with my Bible. Sometimes reading with children around can be distracting, I know, but they'll never forget their parents sitting and reading God's word. I vividly remember my own mom doing this over the years.

We all come from very different places when it comes to scripture. Some of us memorized it in easily digestible bites with little thought to context or bigger meaning. Others heard scripture read aloud in church services throughout our lives, without ever studying them in full. Scripture has been used as a weapon, and certain verses still trigger negative responses for many of us. Maybe you're new to the Bible, and you've really no idea how to begin. Wherever you're coming from, I'm confident the Bible can anchor you to our historic faith, and to the God who inspired it. Hear the strength and confidence the psalmist David expresses, as paraphrased by Eugene Peterson in *The Message*:

> I've already run for dear life straight to the arms of God. So why would I run away now when you say, "Run to the mountains; the evil bows are bent, the wicked arrows aimed to shoot under cover of darkness at every heart open to God. The bottom's dropped out of the country; good people don't have a chance?" But God hasn't moved to the mountains; his holy address hasn't changed. He's in charge, as always. (Psalm 11:1–4)

This assurance that our anchor will hold, even after the bottom drops out, comes from spending time with God in his word. As we've seen, there are lots of ways to do this. Let's take a closer look at the benefits of reading scripture, in all its complexity, in different ways.

CHAPTER 14

Wrestling for a Blessing

When you stop trying to force the Bible to be something it's not—static, perspicacious, certain, absolute—then you're free to revel in what it is: living, breathing, confounding, surprising, and yes, perhaps even magic.

—Rachel Held Evans, *Inspired*

n the twenty-fifth chapter of Genesis, readers are introduced to Jacob and his twin, Esau, who are the sons of Isaac and Rebekah. We know from the few stories that follow their birth, Jacob is favored by his mother, while Esau is favored by his father. Eventually, the two boys part ways and Jacob sets off to find a wife among his parents' people in Haran. Jacob stays there for twenty years, marrying sisters, also having relations with their maids, bearing twelve sons and one daughter. An angel of the Lord visits him, telling him it's time to return home. Time to load up his family, his livestock, and his possessions, and reconnect with his family. Even Esau, with whom he is estranged. The night before he meets up with Esau again, a man (other translations say angel) wrestles with him until daybreak. Jacob did not give in, even throwing his hip out. The man says, "Let me go." Jacob responds, "I will not let you go, unless you bless me" (Genesis 32:26). And so the man did bless him.

Did Jacob wrestle with a man, as we read in the story, or with God? If we read closely, Jacob later says, "For I have seen God face to face, and yet my life is preserved" (Genesis 32:30). We can know this for sure: Jacob leaves the wrestling match a changed man.

For some, the Bible is just another book. Mere words on a page. For a Christian, the Old and New Testaments are a way to see God and Jesus, metaphorically speaking, but the task isn't always easy. Some things in scripture ring clear. Other times, it becomes a wrestling match. What does a challenging passage tell us about God? What did Jesus mean by that particular parable? We can know, because Jacob taught us, keep wrestling, refuse to let go, and God will bless you.

I read every verse every year. In February, when it's still snowing in Michigan, our chronological Bible group makes its way through Leviticus. I don't find it boring (anymore), but it still leaves me with plenty of questions.

In the twenty-first chapter of Leviticus, Moses is giving the priests some instructions the Lord has for them, such as this one: give the following instructions to Aaron, "No descendant of Aaron the priest who has a blemish [other translations use "defect"] shall come near to offer the Lord's offerings by fire; since he has a blemish he shall not come near to offer the food of his God" (Leviticus 21:21).

Our online reading group has a woman who was born disfigured on the right side of her body. She's one of the smartest women I know and can preach a mighty sermon. Another man has cerebral palsy, and he's a gifted musician, songwriter, and a Methodist pastor. But in the Old Testament times, if they had been in the Aaronic line of priests, they could not approach the altar to offer the special gifts of food to God. Why? I do not know. It felt extremely uncomfortable to read, then discuss, it with them.

Using every research skill I possessed, I've found articles from both Jewish and Christian scholars addressing the question. They offer some suggestions but nothing that makes the discomfort go away. Nothing that makes it seem fair. If I didn't know God better, I'd say he was being a jerk, but I know there's more. I sit with our online group, with these two friends in particular, and I ask God to show himself to us in this.

I've never answered my "why" definitively. Wrestling with this passage has given me greater sensitivity to disabled individuals in the body of Christ. It keeps me on the lookout for ways to include everyone.

In her book *Forgiving God*, Hilary Yancey writes about her experience as a first-time mom, finding out her son has complex physical disabilities. In struggling with the diagnosis, then the reality of caring for her son, Yancey had a lot of questions for God, and sometimes it all fell to silence. Eventually, though, she's able to reimagine God, and in that process, she finds more of him. I'm thankful she shared her story.

She writes: "But if we imagine that this knowledge God has about things we do not know is more like God seeing, God standing somewhere and understanding things we haven't yet learned, I wonder if this might give us room to breathe."

Early one fall, I met up with a pastor friend to attend Western Theological Seminary's Friday morning chapel service. He told me I would enjoy it, and on Fridays they serve communion. The service was not lengthy, but it was rich in liturgy. The weekly time together includes responsive readings, a number of songs, a short message, and then the call to prepare our hearts for communion. The woman leading chapel that day explained they had tried a new gluten-free, dairy-free, nut-free bread recipe. There were two goblets, with one offering wine and the other grape juice. They made a great deal of effort to accommodate every person looking to partake in communion. As this thought entered my mind, I saw three individuals get up from their seats in the front row. They retrieved a pitcher, and one poured water into a basin while the others held it. Participants could dip their hands in this water before proceeding to the bread and wine. Although it was slight, I could see that these three worship leaders had varying levels of disability. My friend later explained to me that the seminary has an apartment complex where students live alongside young adults with cognitive disabilities. These young adults were the residents helping to serve communion that day.

My mind went immediately to this difficult passage in Leviticus. Christ came to restore all things, and while I'm still not sure of all that Leviticus was teaching the people of God, I know it was good and true to dip my hands in the holy water held up by these men and women with disabilities. I caught a vision for what our churches can be, and how we all benefit when we see one another as we are and make an effort to be considerate of everyone.

In conclusion, sometimes when we read a section of the Bible, we can feel as if God has a specific word for us. Your right path might come as you're reading some obscure passage in Jeremiah, for example, and you sense it was God directing you, and not only your mind coming up with an answer. Other times, it's not so clear. Much of scripture remains a mystery, no matter how much time I spend reading it. It can truly be a wrestling match, but one God blesses, sometimes with deeper wisdom, other times with a sense of his peace in the midst of the unknown. The honesty with which I can approach the scriptures refreshes me. Maybe that's the greater purpose.

CHAPTER 15

Knowing God

Over the years I have wrestled with scripture, argued and learned from different colleagues, preachers, and scholars, and settled into an understanding of the Bible as a collection of inspired and extraordinary texts that rehearse the spiritual experiences of two ancient faith communities— Jews and Christians—and all the tensions, conflicts, and struggles within and between them.

—Diana Butler Bass, *Freeing Jesus*

My first "big girl" Bible has the year 1981 written in it in my mother's handwriting. I wouldn't have dared to mark in the pages of scripture, but I did fill out the front where it asked for baptism date, church camp experiences, and other notable faith formation moments. I saved poems from bulletin inserts. It's a memento of my childhood days in the church. I regularly carried my Bible to church, and took sermon notes from a young age, but I never really sat down and read the Bible. Like other churchgoing children, I cut my quiet time teeth on devotionals. They would include a verse at the beginning, share a few thoughts on that verse, and end with a prayer.

For many of us, we start out reading scripture because we know it's important, but it can be boring if we aren't taught how to make a connection. If we keep going, through the boredom, and make reading the Bible a habit, we notice a progression. At first, I went from recognizing a scattering of individual verses, to the beginning stages of piecing it all together, to studying everything I could get my hands on, and then after years of interaction, I've reached a sweet spot. God and I sit down to read the Bible together. He might give me an "aha" moment, or I might simply sense his presence ever so slightly, and it's the sweetest thing. My pastor calls this the chocolate cake stage. For me, a flourless chocolate cake with raspberry sauce then—calories don't count.

Psalm 119 is all about delighting in God's law, realizing it exists for our benefit. I appreciate all I was taught about meditating on God's law, and being encouraged to fix my eyes on his ways (Psalm 119:15). Although I wish I had understood more about the fullness of the Bible story as a child, I am thankful for the verses I memorized. They're still here inside of me. Today, I encourage people to memorize larger sections at a time, rather than a single verse. This aids in comprehension of context, whom a prophet was addressing, what Jesus was doing before and after a certain passage, or the heart of Paul's letter to a particular church. It's also a gift to be able to recite passages, letting your mind focus on the things of God, as a calming method when things get stressful. I've seen popular teachers like Beth Moore move into scripture memorization methods like this, even entire books, and it makes a lot of sense to me.

I have a number of Bibles in a variety of translations and paraphrases and use them in rotation. There's a Sunday church Bible, a teaching Bible for when I have our fourth- and fifth-grade students, a daily reading Bible, a psalm-reading Bible, and at least one Bible-study-teaching Bible. I like the way a variety keeps me alert, often providing unfamiliar phrasing or words for a verse I know well in a different translation.

Much like I rely on a variety of translations, I've learned to utilize a variety of exercises to interact with scripture. Here are a few methods to try, and any of them could be done by reading out loud too (maybe don't try it this way in a crowded room of people). Read the words of Jesus, sometimes in red letters, all the way through. Read a chapter in Proverbs each day for a month, as there are thirty-one chapters. Read a chapter, start with Genesis one, if you'd like, more than once in a single setting. Use ancient methods like *lectio divina* and imaginative prayer to see what God might show you. Read a whole epistle in one sitting.

I often do this last one myself. I research the recipient of the letter first, jotting down notes in my Bible or in a notebook. If it's recognized as a letter from Paul, I reference the order of his letters. When did he write this one? If the letter is addressed to a church, I study the city where it's located. Where was it on a map? Does the city still exist by that name today? Was the population Jewish or Gentile or mixed? Where else is the city mentioned in scripture? Once I've learned some about the city, then I read the letter out loud. I better understand the letter because I've learned about its context. I sense the emotion of the author. Taking these initial steps, and reading the words out loud, gives the words greater meaning.

No matter what method you use, I've learned we get the most out of scripture when we approach it as a way God reveals himself to us. What can we learn about God in the stories we find there? How does God show up in the overall narrative? And as we better know God, we can better know ourselves. I like what Paul wrote in his letter to the church at Ephesus, about what he knew to be true about God: "Now to him who by the power at work within us is able to accomplish abundantly far more than all we can ask or imagine, to him be glory in the church and in Christ Jesus to all generations, forever and ever. Amen" (Ephesians 3:20–21).

Every step along the way, reading the Bible helps us become more Christlike. This is it. When reading the Bible regularly, and putting other spiritual practices in place, becomes our rhythm, shaky ground doesn't feel so shaky. We might not consciously recognize all the changes it's making in us, but the formation is happening. God's power is at work, accomplishing more than we can ever realize. I'm often surprised when others mention spiritual growth they've seen in me, and I've not even realized it yet myself.

I've also learned God's people can read the same Bible and reach different conclusions. I can take parts of the Bible literally and someone else might take them figuratively, and we both still find God. Debates over these things are important, but if we get lost in them, we can miss the big picture God longs for us to see. By spending time in the Bible, we can know God.

Let me repeat that because I cannot get over it. By spending time in the Bible, we can know God. Of course, there are other ways to know him too. I haven't always realized the importance of learning about God in all the ways. This has grown in importance to me. We're always looking to strike a balance. Sometimes I learn more about God by listening to the Holy Spirit directly, not having scripture in front of me at the time. I have learned a lot about Jesus by getting to know other brothers and sisters who follow him. Nature and science are excellent tools for learning about God. Studying ancient Judaism and Middle Eastern, African and European cultures has helped me understand the historical contexts God was working in when scripture was written and compiled. Learning about church traditions points me to godly worship.

In order to see God in God's fullness, as much as we can in the here and now, we need to consider all of the ways we can better know God. This certainly includes scripture. If you really want to read about some shaky times, read Judges. In these pages are real men and women, at times striving to be faithful, always stumbling along the way. They have much to teach us about being human. In the pages of scripture we find a God who longs to reveal himself to humans, no matter what circumstances we find ourselves in at any given moment. By spending time in the Bible, we can know God.

CHAPTER 16

Pray the Scriptures

O Heavenly King, the Comforter, the Spirit of Truth, who art
in all places and fillest all things, Treasury of blessings and
giver of life: come and dwell in us, cleanse us from every
stain, and save our souls, O gracious Lord.

—Orthodox Prayer to the Holy Spirit

'm not sure if this chapter fits in with the prayer section or the scripture section. When using resources like prayer books, the lines
between scripture and formal prayers get blurred, because the
men and women who compiled these prayer books, often under
the umbrella of specific church traditions, took great care to weave
passages of scripture into the prayers.

Episcopalians and Anglicans have called their volumes a Book
of Common Prayer since the first book was written by Thomas
Cranmer and published in 1549. Whether the 1662 Book still
officially in use by the Church of England, the 1979 Book used by
the Episcopal Church, or any number of other prayer books from
member churches within the Anglican Communion (that confed-
eration of churches connected to the Church of England and the
Archbishop of Canterbury), it is a fixture of prayer and worship for
Anglicans and Episcopalians, including prayers for both corporate
and individual use. I have personally found a number of spiritual
treasures in its pages.

Incorporating the practice of praying with prayer books into
my daily routine jarred me a little. I'd largely been taught to study
scripture, learning exegetical techniques designed to draw meaning

from passages. When I only read the Bible this way, sometimes it felt as if there was a disconnect between my Bible reading and my spirit. Sometimes we read the Bible to engage our minds, but that's different than letting it sink into one's soul. Eugene Peterson speaks of this in his book, *Eat This Book:* "But exegesis is focused attention, asking questions, sorting through possible meanings. Exegesis is rigorous, disciplined, intellectual work. It rarely feels 'spiritual.'"

It was about five years ago that I added formal prayers to my own routine. For the first time I was reading some of the same prayers and passages on repeat. Certain phrases would jump off the page, feeling powerful in a new way. As I grew more familiar with it, I could anticipate what was coming next in the prayer. It was as if I was being carried in a type of forward motion.

It wasn't only the phrases of these prayer books that traveled with me throughout my day; the presence of the Holy Spirit felt stronger too. I'd invited him to the forefront and there he stood, guiding my every step. Alternating between a variety of poetry and traditional prayer books, I found the books reflect the person or tradition from whence they come. If I used Phyllis Tickle's books on praying the divine hours, I got an Anglican feel to my prayer time. I likened it to how I felt when reading the Book of Common Prayer. If I used the *Valley of Vision*, a Puritan collection of prayers, I noted an emphasis on a sinful nature, and our great need for God to save us, but also a weaving of words that wraps my soul in comfort first thing in the morning. Poetry books, like *Accompanied by Angels: Poems of the Incarnation*, by Luci Shaw, showcase the intimacy of an Evangelical Protestant.

My next prayer book purchase will be a book exploring Celtic spirituality. In ancient times, these Christians in northwestern Europe weren't as influenced by Roman culture, secular or religious. One poem from that tradition, St. Patrick's "The Breastplate," is particularly meaningful to me. Revel in all those prepositions. Here is a portion of it:

Christ with me, Christ before me, Christ behind me,
Christ in me, Christ beneath me, Christ above me,

Christ on my right, Christ on my left,

Christ when I lie down, Christ when I sit down, Christ
when I arise,

Christ in the heart of every man who thinks of me,

Christ in the mouth of everyone who speaks of me,

Christ in every eye that sees me,

Christ in every ear that hears me.

There are any number of prayer books to help create a natural rhythm of praying to God. Prayer books have been written by individuals and small groups and by denominational committees. Some are newly composed, and others bring centuries of other pray-ers along with them. Many have a set structure to their pages, following daily or hourly patterns and suggesting patterns of scripture readings, called lectionaries. I've even seen a website dedicated to a Baptist prayer book. What a great way to get to know one another, by understanding the topics, methodology, and focus of our prayers.

In addition to prayer books, practices like *lectio divina* offer us a contemplative method for communing with God using scripture. Slowly, I'm learning how to do this, and how it feels different than exegetical study. Here are two real-life examples.

A few years ago, I attended a writers' conference where the facilitator took us through a spiritual exercise using *lectio divina*. In our prayer exercise, Ed read the twenty-third psalm, a psalm of David, out loud multiple times. As he began reading, my initial response was, "I already know this." My mind raced ahead, trying to beat him to the finish line by saying the next verse before he did. So much for contemplation.

The second time through, my mind shifted and I started trying to recollect when David had written this psalm. Was he on the run from King Saul? Was it accompanied by stringed instruments in the temple days? I'm a Bible study teacher through and through, so my mind went to hermeneutics. That's all good, but it's not really meditation. I struggled to remove the analytical thoughts from my mind.

Finally, about three or four times into the recitation of Psalm 23, my mind stilled. I honed in on the words. Only the words. It was like they had a life of their own: real, breathing life. I smiled at the idea of God preparing a table for me, for I love a well-prepared table of food. At the end of the exercise, our facilitator asked if there was a phrase that stuck out to us in the reading. A certain idea God had for us. He encouraged us to spend a few minutes praying about that phrase.

I shall not want.

How unoriginal; I got stuck on the first line, but it was God's word to me. Here I was at a retreat where I didn't feel like I belonged. There were published authors and other writers who had been doing this a lot longer than me. God wanted me to hear it loud and clear—God is writing my story. I shall not want theirs. So, one by one, I shared with God some of the areas of my life where I did want something, and I gave them to him.

It began to occur to me in a very real way, maybe this is exactly how the psalms are intended to be read; slowly, prayerfully, out loud, on repeat. I began to practice *lectio divina* with the psalms more regularly in my own life.

I realized I had made this spiritual practice a personal tool when my church experienced a great tragedy. We had a worship leader whose singing took you right to the foot of the cross. Natalie stood no more than four-foot-eleven, but she sang big for Jesus. He'd given her a new heart, figuratively and literally, years before she joined our church family. One ordinary Sunday morning, her heart didn't seem to be working quite right. She didn't sing that morning, and had her husband take her to the hospital instead. They admitted her right away. Nat didn't leave that hospital the same way she'd entered it. She left her earthly body behind as her spirit entered its eternal home.

Natalie and I had a special bond, as we were both Bible teachers. We loved God's word and the women who studied it with us.

Her group of ladies met on Wednesday mornings, and Natalie had died earlier in the week. I felt it was important that I meet with those ladies who still wanted to gather. They knew, as I did, Natalie wouldn't want us to forsake the gathering together of believers. I got to the classroom early, putting a few boxes of Kleenex around the room, and spent time in prayer, asking God to give me the words of comfort these ladies needed.

He gave me *lectio divina*, and no one could have been more surprised than I was to realize this. In this time of deep grief, the ladies didn't need to learn a new thing. They didn't need a lot of words. They needed to be together, joined together by the common thread that brought them there week after week. We turned to a familiar Bible passage (I cannot for the life of me remember which one) and I read it out loud one time, two times, three times. I didn't use the term for what we were doing (it might have been construed as Catholic and I wasn't prepared to go there in my explanation). After the readings, we discussed what verses jumped out at us. The women wove in stories of Natalie. We laughed. We cried. I cannot think of a way for scripture to provide more comfort than the method we used to read it together that September morning. We remembered her together. We read our Bibles together. We always will.

CHAPTER 17

Getting to Know Mary

"Before I took pen in hand," she writes, "I knelt down before the statue of the Blessed Virgin, which had given to my family so many proofs of her maternal protection, and I begged her to guide my hand and not allow me to write a single line that might displease her."

—St. Thérèse of Lisieux

grew up believing Catholics worshiped Mary. This was not something I tried to understand, it's just something I "knew." I never gave understanding it a second thought because we were only supposed to worship the three members of the Trinity: Father, Son, and Holy Spirit. Could you even be a legitimate Christian and worship Mary? As for the Orthodox Christian tradition, which also emphasizes the adoration and veneration of Mary, I'd never even heard of them.

Of all the things I've learned in getting to know the larger Church, these pat answers I had are what shame me the most. I grew up in a conservative, evangelical American culture, which gifted me with plenty of pat answers. I also knew if I studied the Bible hard enough, heard enough lengthy sermon series, and read approved books, I would have the right answers. It's not exactly like this, but it's enough so to make me squirm these days—I thought with the right kind of resources and enough time and commitment on my part, I could figure God out.

I thought we should mostly mention Mary at Christmas, maybe Easter, and usually with her name being part of a pair—Mary and Joseph. I see things differently now. When I realize another Christian has a different spiritual practice than I do, such as venerating Mary, I ask myself how I might benefit from learning about why they do this certain thing. I inquire of the Holy Spirit how understanding this practice can teach me more about God and the body of Christ.

Harp of Glory: Enzira Sebhat is an alphabetical hymn of prose for the ever-blessed virgin Mary from the Ethiopian Orthodox Church. Upon hearing about this book, I found it easily on the publisher's website, and it arrived in my mailbox in a few days. For several months, I'd read a few pages from this book first thing each morning.

There was a time when I would have never touched a book like this, but I'm growing. The Ethiopian church tradition dates back approximately to the days of the book of Acts. In the eighth chapter of that book, Luke tells a story of an Ethiopian eunuch in the court of Candace (the Ethiopian name for queen), who Philip the evangelist came across on a wilderness road. The Ethiopian was reading Isaiah and not understanding it (and here we find ourselves thousands of years later still trying to understand it). When Philip asked if he was comprehending what he was reading, the Ethiopian replied he couldn't without a guide. Philip put on his evangelism hat and proclaimed the good news. Then, check out what happened next.

> As they were going along the road, they came to some water; and the eunuch said, "Look, here is water! What is to prevent me from being baptized?" (Acts 8:36)

Church tradition tells us the Ethiopian went back home and shared his own good news about the gospel (literally "good news"). St. John Chrysostom, a fourth-century church father from Antioch, mentions in his writings there were Ethiopians in the crowd at Pentecost, which we read about in the second chapter of Acts, so it's possible there was already a church forming there before the eunuch returned home. From these earliest days, the Ethiopian Orthodox Church plays an important role in church history and today, they have the second-highest number of Orthodox Christians worldwide, thirty-six million people.

If I humble myself enough, could a Christian tradition numbering thirty-six million people have something to teach me, not only about Mary, or Theotokos (God-bearer) as she's known by the Orthodox, but about our God they've been worshipping since the earliest days of the church? In a book about finding sources of strength during our most difficult days, it seems important to acknowledge that millions of Christians find great comfort in praying to Mary. They value the prayers of the saints, and while I'm still working to understand how that fits, I'm listening and learning. Here's what I learned about Mary:

One summer day, early in the morning, before my household awakened for the day, I opened *Harp of Glory*. I read the introduction, as any real lover of books should (there was no acknowledgment section, I checked). The introduction spoke of an ecumenical sadness over the fact that Ethiopian spirituality remains an unknown element to many Christians. "It might be a more appropriate thing to think more generously of the great antiquity and profound spirituality of the worlds of the Coptic and Ethiopic churches, arenas of Christian life and deeply tested experience, for these churches are veritable cradles of martyrs."

Before reading any further, I bowed my head to pray, repenting of my vainglorious Christianity. Then, I began reading the hymn. Each section begins with descriptive phrases in the name of God the Father, God the Son, and God the Holy Spirit. At the bottom of each page, scripture references are cited. A mind-blowing number of citations, found in the eighty-one books of the Ethiopian Bible, a translation nearly eight hundred years older than the King James Version.

The author of this hymn loves Mary, and regularly includes her in daily worship practices. The hymn passes every scripture litmus test I know. Christians who interact with this hymn certainly believe in a triune God. The gospel of Christ is clearly represented.

A few months into reading this book-length hymn, Nicole Roccas, a writer friend, who has stepped into the fullness of the Orthodox tradition, shared these thoughts on Twitter:

> The Mother of God + me = it's complicated. . . . Context: venerating Mary has never come easily or naturally to me. I used to credit this to my Protestant upbringing, but beneath all the doctrine and dogma, it probably boils down to the fact that I just don't like being mothered very much. It's awkward, risky, and cramps my fierce independence. Don't get me wrong, I believe all the things about the Mother of God, I just would rather not ask her (or pretty much anyone) for help.

I told Nicole about the book I'd been using in my morning devotions and shared with her what I had learned. Using figurative language, the author likens Mary metaphorically to any and every vessel that's ever carried a holy object on behalf of God's people.

> My Lady Mary—Sacred Ark of the Tablets of the
> Commandments,
> Shaded by the covering wings of the Cherubim . . .
> Accept my prayer as if it were a libation of wine and other gifts
> And enable it to rise up on my behalf into the heavenly court
> of your Son.

Nicole got me thinking. She admitted to being fiercely independent. Perhaps this points to the relationship she had with her own parents, her mother in particular. I thought of my own mom, my greatest mentor in the faith. We read of Jesus's first miracle in the second chapter of John. Mary, Jesus, and his disciples attend a wedding in Cana. The wedding party ran out of wine, and Mary knew right where to turn. She informed Jesus they had no wine. He seemingly ignores her, stating his hour had not yet come, but Mary knew her son would help. She turns to the servants, saying, "Do whatever he tells you" (John 2:5).

I'm sure there were things Mary didn't understand, and she never forgot the prophecy that her soul would be pierced by a sword, which Simeon gave to her upon meeting the infant child in the Temple (Luke 2:35). What Mary knew, though, is what my own mom also showed me: we're at our best when we do whatever Jesus tells us to do.

For some of you, the influence of one or both of your parents on your faith is not a healthy one. Looking beyond faith, you might have learned at an early age, if you were going to survive in this world, the only person you could really trust was you. In the words of the tradition in which I grew up, perhaps you've given your life to Jesus, but the surrender part and the trusting part are altogether unfamiliar to you. And that's to say nothing of trusting other people. We long for connection, but too often it has come at a price. There's a great deal of courage involved. Coming to peace with how you were parented, and the impact of other relationships you've had, is a part of growing into adulthood in life and in faith. In my own life, I've had to examine what helped me grow in my dependence on Christ (and those in the church) and what led me to protect myself from the vulnerability required to place that kind of trust in a higher power, in other people too. Along the way, God gives us spiritual parents, biological or not, as well as brothers and sisters. This. This is what it means to be a part of the family of God, and it does require taking some risks.

We need mother figures, from the pages of scripture, throughout history, in our present lives, who show us how to live a faithful life. Mary saw Jesus's miracles, healings, death, and resurrection firsthand. Looking at my own mother's life of faithfulness, I have seen the ways God has cared for her, a widow. Miracles big and small. Practicing my own faith doesn't feel as awkward or risky because these women inspire me to remain in him. Let's be clear: neither Mary the mother of Jesus nor my own mother had what any of us might consider an easy life. Both knew pain and suffering;

both felt the ground quake beneath their feet, as their lives changed in unforeseen ways. It is not because of a lack of sorrow in their lives that they provide this model for me. Mary—and those mother figures in your own life—can serve as a trustworthy guide precisely because she knows the anguish we feel.

Are there Christians who go too far in venerating Mary? Possibly, but who decides? Are there other Christians who undervalue Mary? Those of us who have never heard the Magnificat (Mary's prayer found in Luke 1) as an Advent hymn or realized its powerful statement of solidarity? It seems some of us could show more respect to the woman God chose to bear his son. She who without hesitation said yes. How beautiful to help one another better understand Mary and her place in the gospel story.

Here's my point, and it's what I told my Orthodox friend when she shared she didn't feel comfortable venerating Mary. I'm getting to know Mary too. I have yet to ask her to pray for me, although if I come to find out she has done so someday, I'll be delighted. In a sermon, Martin Luther, the great reformer, said, "The veneration of Mary is inscribed in the very depths of the human heart."

St. Anthony, an early church father from the Coptic orthodox tradition who lived in the third century, is known for being the first monastic to go dwell in the literal wilderness (the eastern desert of Egypt) to better know God. He said, "I saw the snares that the enemy spreads out over the world, and I said groaning, 'What can get through from such snares?' Then I heard a voice saying to me, 'Humility.'"

In my quest for spiritual practices that grow my faith and ground my life, I'm earnestly seeking. With deep humility, I ask my brothers and sisters in Christ to teach me things they have known for some time. I don't fear learning something wrong. I trust my foundation. May Mary be a guide and source of strength to you as well.

CHAPTER 18

A Reflection on Jesus Calming the Storm

And when he got into the boat, his disciples followed him. A windstorm arose on the sea, so great that the boat was being swamped by the waves; but he was asleep. And they went and woke him up, saying, "Lord, save us! We are perishing!" And he said to them, "Why are you afraid, you of little faith?" Then he got up and rebuked the winds and the sea; and there was a dead calm. They were amazed, saying, "What sort of man is this, that even the winds and the sea obey him?"

—Matthew 8:23–27

opefully you can already see parallels between this Bible story, found in the three synoptic gospels (Matthew, Mark, and Luke), and the storms we face in life, wondering where Jesus is in our tumultous circumstances and if he has in fact fallen asleep again, leaving us to perish, or feel abandoned to sink or swim on our own.

Each account of Jesus calming the storm is relatively short, and they are notably similar. Jesus has been teaching and tells his disciples to get on the boat so they can cross to the other side of the sea. Mark notes there were other boats too. There did not seem to be a storm in the forecast. Isn't that the way of things sometimes? All is going well, everything around you seems fine, until it's not.

Suddenly (a few translations mention this word in Matthew's version, chapter 8, verse 24, and I'm glad because I sense that's a great word for what happens at this moment in scripture), a storm comes up on the water. The boat is filling with water and taking quite a beating. Jesus is asleep. The disciples woke Jesus up, asking for help, "Lord, save us! We are perishing!" (Matthew 8:25). The storm, it appears, was that bad.

Yet Jesus doesn't seem to be in a big hurry. The storm doesn't alarm him. The thing that seems to bother Jesus the most in this moment is the disciples' lack of faith. He told the winds and the storm to settle down, and they did. "There was a dead calm" (Matthew 8:26).

I appreciate that Jesus can calm a storm in an instant if he wants to. The disciples were impressed too. He did it again, you know, calmed another storm. We looked at it earlier, in the imaginative prayer workshop I attended.

Remember, in the storm-calming story we read about in the fourteenth chapter of Matthew, Jesus had stayed behind to pray. In the midst of the disciples' great fear, after the storm was already going strong, he walked out to them.

"Take heart, it is I; do not be afraid," he said (Matthew 14:27). Then, it is only Matthew who records it, Peter asked Jesus if he could come to him. Perhaps Peter remembered this particular storm. The time Jesus was asleep in the boat, but then when the time was right, he woke up and calmed the storm. Remembering what God has done in the past is mighty fodder for faith.

A one-word response from Jesus was all it took: "Come." We don't know how many steps Peter took. Maybe time stood still as the disciples saw his bravery and Jesus beckoned. It can be so hard to keep our eyes on Jesus. Storms are loud and distracting and call for our attention. Eventually, Peter took his eyes off Jesus and began to sink, and Jesus reached out his hand and caught him. They got back in the boat and the wind ceased.

Where have your Peter moments been? Before the storm ceases, when you're in the throes of it, where have you heard Jesus's summons? It may not be very loud but it's undeniable. If you're in the middle of a stormy time right now, take as many steps as you can to Jesus, and when you fall, he'll reach out his hand to catch you. Eventually, the storm will lessen, but you know what you'll have the privilege of remembering? The time you walked on water, in the midst of a storm, to Jesus.

■ ■ ■

Method: When looking at a story found in the gospel, check out all four books; Matthew, Mark, Luke, and John. It helps to know something about the namesakes of these books, and their original audiences. Matthew the tax collector, one of the twelve disciples, writes for a Jewish audience. Mark, friend of Peter and cousin of Barnabas, who we first read about as a follower of Jesus in Acts, wrote for the Romans. Luke, a doctor and a Gentile, who traveled with Paul on his missionary journeys, wrote for the Greeks. John, the beloved, one of Jesus's closest companions among the twelve disciples, wrote for everyone. First, look to see which of the gospels tell the story. Next, read each account in parallel. What details are unique? Where do they agree? Always be asking yourself, What did the gospel writers want their readers to know based on particular stories and details they shared?

Would you pray with me?

God, sudden storms feel scary, and our boats can feel like they're sinking. May this truth settle deep in our hearts, you are the calmer of storms. The winds and the sea still obey you. Amen.

PART IV
FOUNDATION

CHAPTER 19

Look for the Faithful

The mark of a follower of Jesus is following. The mark of a
follower of Jesus is that she or he has given Jesus her or
his heart.

— Scot McKnight, *One.Life*

Mister Rogers's mother regularly reminded him to "look for the helpers"
in times of crisis, and this is still all-around sound advice for
each of us. I hear it quoted often. It's good to "look for the
helpers" when we are in crisis—and to discover the joy of "being
the helper" when we are able to provide that support to another.

As we enter our daughter's teenage years, I'm encouraging her
to do the same. When it comes to the development of her faith, I'd
change the phrasing a little. I want her to build a life where she is
not only helpful, but faithful.

What do I mean by a life of faithfulness? I look to those people regularly seeking God through many of the spiritual practices
we've mentioned in this book, and others. Like all of us, they have
faced crises, and they know the world can be a cruel, hard place.
Again and again, they rise up and lift their heads. We watch them
do it. And in doing so, they encourage us to do the same.

The spiritual practices we might use ebb and flow. It's true,
my daughter's faith experience doesn't look like mine. Sometimes
I think her practices should look a certain way (more scripture

memorization, more hymns), and God reminds me, he is calling her to him. Even though shaky ground looks even shakier when we involve our children in the equation, I trust God to finish the work he has begun in her. We can trust him to do this in our lives too.

From that right perspective, I note the spiritual practices she is learning. She shares about her prayer life with me, and I hear how it is growing. Together, we've learned a lot about seeking God in the silence. She reads her Bible regularly and helps pick out her devotions.

This is all good, but I sense God asking me to dig deeper, for there's more I need to realize. What do I mean when I say I want her to be faithful? In a conversation with a friend, it finally clicks. When it comes to growing in the faith and finding those "helpers" with whom to surround ourselves in times of crisis, the faithful are our guides. They're out there, only a step or two ahead of us, showing us what real and lasting change Jesus makes in a Christian's life.

I've also seen evidence of the good exhibited in the lives of those of other faiths. Although I haven't had the honor of having a Jewish friend in real life, social media has connected me with several men and women I'd be delighted to meet in person someday. They share their stories, often with photos, about their own spiritual practices, including the festivals they participate in on an annual basis. I've learned about some of their struggles, things we struggle with as well. I'm thankful for what they're teaching me about their own faith. At times, it seems we have forgotten how to befriend one another. Author Shawn Smucker wrote a book about a friendship he forged with a Syrian refugee who is a Muslim. *Once We Were Strangers* is a beautiful look at how we can walk alongside one another, even in all of our diversity. He writes: "No matter how different they are, they share many of the same concerns, the same hopes. I hear them all laugh again, and I wonder what it is that keeps us frightened of each other."

Turning again to our Christian faith, more than knowing a particular spiritual practice, I want my daughter to know Jesus; to be a helper like he was when he walked this earth. I want her to be a woman of great faith.

Faithful like my friend Janet. When I first started going to my current church, Janet and her husband, Lee, were older friends. They have been faithful members of our church plant since the beginning. Over the years Janet and I have studied the Bible, discussed books, and sang hymns (the alto line) together. A few years ago, Lee was diagnosed with dementia. As his health declined, Janet had to make difficult decisions about his care. Fortunately, she had family who walked through this with her. Making many of these difficult decisions while the world was under quarantine, it was a season of emotional turmoil for them. Lee passed away not long ago. After Lee died, we didn't see Janet at church for a while. I would text her hymn lyrics from time to time, and check in with her. She explained needing this time to be alone with God. In her early days of grief, she'd see her family regularly, but the ordinary days were spent with her and God. She needed to rest in him, to heal from her grief.

Months later, Janet and I got together for lunch. She talked about her time alone with God. She mentioned a next-door neighbor, who had been a great companion, a helper as well. Then, she told me a story about one of her final, intimate moments with Lee. With her permission, I share it with you. She went to see Lee in the rest home they'd found for him. He was lucid that afternoon, which always felt like such a gift. After praying and reading scripture together, Janet retrieved some bread and juice she'd brought with her. As one of our church elders, Lee had served her communion many times. This time, she served him. Husband and wife, in Christ. All those years of walking together with Christ as their head, ready to catch the other should they fall. And you know there were seasons when the bottom seemed to drop out. We all have them. This communion felt like a celebration of their faithful life in these final moments, when, for the first time, she served him communion, and a circle of partnership felt even more sacred.

Or like my friend Kate. She's in her forties and married to a pastor-turned-mission-director. Joshua is from Nigeria and regularly travels to Africa on behalf of the mission he has started there. They have four children, ages eight to fifteen, and Kate manages things on her own when Joshua is out of town. A bit of shakiness (and craziness) in the everyday chaos, I'm certain. Kate and I have discussed this work, with her husband spending a lot of time out of the country, and how difficult it can be for her. She's proud of Joshua though. "I really want to be a good missionary wife," she says. What I hope she sees is that she is.

In addition to supporting Joshua, Kate works at a local school. She's active politically. She serves at her local church. Kate has her regular spiritual practices, but they always drive her to action. I admire her strength, and the tireless commitment she has to making this world a better place. Together this couple is making a difference locally and globally. I can't wait to see how their kids serve God, like they've seen their faithful parents do.

It's not certain practices, and it's certainly not particular labels, I want to pass on to my daughter, it's a way of life as a disciple of Jesus—what the earliest Christ-followers called The Way. A faithful life of obedience she hopefully sees in me, and in the people of God we meet, who can help her turn to Jesus during those times after the bottom drops out of her own life. Holy, godly people are the most solid people I know. In the words of Paul: "And so while there has never been any question about your honesty in these matters—I couldn't be more proud of you!—I want you also to be smart, making sure every 'good' thing is the *real* thing. Don't be gullible in regard to smooth-talking evil. Stay alert like this, and before you know it the God of peace will come down on Satan with both feet, stomping him into the dirt. Enjoy the best of Jesus!" (Romans 16:19–20, MSG)

CHAPTER 20

More to Learn

It is possible for us to live in the very sense of the Lord's
presence, under even the most difficult circumstances.

— Brother Lawrence

woman by the name of Hildegard, a twelfth-century Benedictine
abbess in Bingen, Germany, stood ahead of her time in many
categories. She emphasized a healthy diet, practicing moder-
ation and rest, and the use of herbs for medicinal purposes. She
wrote books and music. A quote from Hildegard caught my eye as
I researched her: "Even in a world that's being shipwrecked, remain
brave and strong." Shaky then, shaky now.

According to Hildegard, the goal in developing spiritual disciplines is realizing this: "The mystery of God hugs you in its all-
encompassing arms."

Learning more about the history of the church, the faithful
men and women who have gone before us, has helped me understand that there's never been a time without upheaval and tragedy.
It's not a better time or place we're seeking, but a deeper understanding of the security we have in Christ. Hard times are hard,
and we will experience calamity and catastrophe. But we will not
face these things alone.

There are ways to walk with Jesus that I'm just beginning to
know. I had my own evangelical practices: Bible study, devotional

reading, spontaneous prayer. What I've discovered is I can bring these along as I discover new things. What I thought might alter my Christianity into something false and unrecognizable has deepened it. These gifts from other church traditions and from other people of faith throughout the centuries, carrying such lofty identifying terms as spiritual practices, spiritual disciplines, sacraments, and mysteries, exist for our benefit. They are vehicles to help us move ever closer to God, and they've been helping men and women grow deeper in their faith walks for ages. We're not looking for an out-of-this-world experience every time we use a practice like the Examen or centering prayer, although there have been mystics throughout history who have had such experiences.

Much like the disciplines of healthy eating and physical exercise, we develop a healthier spirituality over time as we work these practices into our daily routine. We look to dietitians and trainers for guidance in the areas of physical health. When it comes to spiritual instruction, there are professionals, in addition to clergy and lay leaders, to help with that too. Spiritual directors can partner with the practices you've already got in place and help you identify what might be hindering your progress. In the Christian life, we hear the admonition, die to self. This means we focus on God first, then view our lives, and our relationships, through that lens. Spiritual directors can help us do this in a healthy way. In fact, Hildegard herself served as a spiritual director. Many would say she still does through her books, letters, and music we have. People in her day recognized her as a faithful disciple and sought her guidance.

In community, whether that includes professionals or not, whether we're physically or spiritually present to one another, we form habits of regularly turning to Jesus. If an old way starts to feel stale, ask God if there's a benefit in continuing this practice, or if it's time to add something new. When your spirit starts to miss the old way, consider bringing it back in. Remember, spiritual practices are not about conjuring up emotions, although sometimes great emotion will occur. They are about developing a life of obedience, training our minds and spirits to rely on Jesus Christ. It's not about checking off a spiritual checklist. It's God who has gifted us with a variety of practices to move us into the fullness of God's love available to us in Christ (Ephesians 3:19).

Exploring these new methods has required two things from me. First, I've had to lay down my assumptions about how God could be found, and realize there will always be more of him beyond my knowing. What I mean by that is what Paul wrote to the Corinthians in the days of the early church, "For now we see in a mirror, dimly, but then we will see face to face. Now I know only in part; then I will know fully, even as I have been fully known" (1 Corinthians 13:12). We cannot fully know God yet, but he is worthy of our pursuit.

Second, I've had to let go of fear. In most of my years as a believer, I was afraid of learning a wrong theology. I was afraid if I prayed with a rosary or gazed prayerfully at an icon, I'd be worshipping an object. I've found instead that these things help our minds enter into a sacred space of prayer. They often help our restless bodies focus.

A word of caution as you implement new-to-you spiritual practices. Sometimes when we learn something new, it makes a big impact, and we can grow bitter over not knowing it sooner. We might think, if I had been aware of this way of knowing God instead of the way it was presented to me, I wouldn't have had to undo the years of wrong thinking that did so much damage. Pride can even enter these thoughts, forgetting we're all growing at the pace God would have for us. God uses those things in our past, as he's using the spiritual practices we're learning to implement now. God is always active in our lives. Grace upon grace, and that includes for yourself.

And it's true. We can weaponize theology, spiritual practices, even our churches. What's important to realize is this happens from all sides. As I often say, if you found catechism class boring, if you only every rotely repeated the Lord's Prayer rather than slowly praying it to plumb its depths, if you were ostracized by the church for asking one too many questions, it isn't the practice itself, or the entire Church, and it certainly isn't Jesus, we should blame. I regularly ask God to prepare my heart for receiving the good in the practices I do.

In addition to incorporating spiritual practices into my days, studying the history of the church has been a surprising stabilizer. Throughout this book, I've shared bits of what I've learned from church history, because I'm convinced the faithful of the past have much to teach us still today.

So we continue the holy work of creating spiritual disciplines in order to further connect with God and one another. Over the years, I have grown in knowledge, but there will always be things I don't know. Things I don't fully understand. I'm always learning. That's faith. Hildegard was right, embracing the mysteries of God has in many ways felt like a divine hug.

CHAPTER 21

Going Wider

What a fellowship, what a joy divine, Leaning on the everlasting arms;
What a blessedness, what a peace is mine, Leaning on the
everlasting arms.

—Elisha A. Hoff, "Leaning on the Everlasting Arms"

My writer friend, Phoebe Farag Mikhail, had an essay in my first book. She was born in Egypt and is a Coptic Orthodox Christian. I deeply appreciate having faith conversations with Phoebe because she offers me a perspective I may not have considered, and she's especially articulate about her beliefs. Often, right in the middle of a conversation, Phoebe will share a quote or a story about an early church father or mother. It's always helpful advice from a faithful one who has gone before us. In this case, thousands of years before us. Phoebe doesn't talk about them that way, though. She talks about them like they're her next-door neighbor. Men and women whose names I often have to look up on the internet.

This is something I often notice when I read through the Old Testament as well. Everyone refers back to the patriarchs, for example, as if they were alive only a generation before the current day.

I've read a few books written by scholars of medieval Christianity. They talk about women like Julian of Norwich and Margery Kempe as if they know them. They've immersed themselves in this period and thus, these Christians who lived all those years ago are their friends on the path.

Fiction opens up the ordinary days of faith for us in a way non-fiction often doesn't. Here's an example of a devout woman relying on ritual and a woman of the Bible to recover her strength after a tragedy. In *Lights on the Mountain*, by Cheryl Anne Tuggle, a young woman named Galina Morozov, who goes by Gracie for short, marries a farmer named Jesse. The author walks her readers through the inside of a Russian Orthodox church, gives details about the couple's traditional wedding, and informs readers about various Russian traditions in the home. I was introduced to a practice of lighting beeswax candles and oil lamps to pray, also prayers of devotion before icons. Gracie suffers a miscarriage, not through any fault of her own, and goes to confession. The author explains Gracie sees this time as a "chance to dust off her soul." Although there were other seasons and ways to take a spiritual inventory, that particular autumn, being in the church, hearing the chanted readings, standing in the confession line, Gracie was able to find her focus. She brought God her sorrow and her longing to have a child. There, with a mind at ease, she prays: "Restore unto me the joy of Thy salvation."

After confessing the burdens she carried, she went to light a candle before the icon of Anna, the Holy Virgin's mother. "Her request to St. Anna was the usual one, the same petition she had been making for years, but this time she did it with freshened faith."

I'm taking inventory of who or what comes to mind when I have faith conversations. It's a good exercise for all of us, perhaps, from time to time. Hopefully, for me, men and women from scripture come to mind, as I spend a fair amount of time in God's word each day. Some might quote a reformer such as Martin Luther, John Calvin, or later, John Wesley. Do our lists span time and tradition? Others may find that mystics such as Hildegard or more contemporary saints such as Dorothy Day or Thomas Merton are their companions. Are there people in a variety of church traditions, ages, genders, and ethnicities? I hope this challenges you to expand your sources. Every person listed here encountered the difficulties of standing on shaky ground, often ground we're still tilling today. This is the universal Church that's greater than we can possibly comprehend. It's done my faith a whole lot of good to realize we're a part of something bigger than ourselves.

I want to know global church history well enough that all sorts of names pop up when I'm talking about Church. This was not my experience growing up in an evangelical church. Some people joke they thought church history started in the 1500s with the reformers. I don't recall ever considering when church history began. I guess I thought we jumped straight from the time of the Acts of the Apostles to circa 1960. I'm not convinced I'm alone in my ignorance. I teach the children in our church, and I carry a children's book on church history in my Bible bag. On the Sundays we get done early with our Bible lesson, I take the opportunity to read the children a church history lesson. I tell them these men and women helped build the church after the Bible times. They are our great-great-great-great-great-great-grandparents, I tell them. A couple of picture books have helped us, the children and me, learn new names like Tertullian and Anne Bradstreet and George Fox. Hopefully we can offer a better understanding of our heritage to the next generation. These ancestors of faith can be such a source of comfort and support. Further, this will go a long way in undoing things like nationalism and denominational elitism.

I wonder sometimes where my ancestors went to church. How did it look different? In what ways is it the same? When I spent those few days at the prayer center, my first silent retreat, I took note of what felt familiar to me and what still felt foreign or "Catholic." I embrace it all more than I used to, but differences still come to mind. Maybe someday I'll stop compartmentalizing altogether. I spent some time in the chapel in the basement of the main building on campus. As I walked in, there was a basin of water at the door, so I dipped my fingers gingerly in the bowl, crossing myself. I noted a statue of Mary and several stations with candles around the room. There was a lectern front and center, with a bookshelf behind it. Worship guides and liturgical books from various church traditions filled the shelves. We have so much to teach one another.

Another afternoon, it was somewhat warm outside. I'd been writing for a few hours and was ready for a lunch break. I walked slowly on the path, contemplating the stations of the cross that had been set up along the way, taking my time but knowing my destination. There's a wooden chapel in the middle of the retreat center, more country than Catholic. The plaque by the front door tells visitors that this is the original chapel of the Franciscan Sisters of the Sacred Heart who arrived in May 1876. They were victims of the German Kulturkampf, a conflict between the Imperial Chancellor Otto von Bismarck and the Roman Catholic Church, as the newly established German Empire sought to subject the church to state control. Shaky ground indeed.

Walking inside, I took in the wooden pews and the altar railing. Universal church furniture if there is such a thing. The silence of the day had fallen all around me, and it met me in this sacred space as well. There's something about a sanctuary. I prayed, my spoken words echoing in the empty space, thankful for what I'm learning. For how God is being revealed in my life and all around me. I walked back down the aisle, closed the wooden screen door behind me, and headed to pick up the lunch I had asked to have prepared. Returning to my cottage, I spent the afternoon writing and reading, nibbling on lunch, and taking a nap. It all felt like prayer to me.

In that Catholic space, a refuge for wandering Christian pilgrims since 1876, our divisions felt entirely beside the point. Men and women of God throughout the ages lived in their own uncertain worlds, and yet lived faithful lives. The more I learn the context of the church in a particular time and place, I find myself asking the same question over and over again: Where can I experience more of Jesus? The next time someone tells you they don't have to be part of a church to be a Christian, go ahead and agree with them. Participation in a church is not, by itself, a salvific act. I pray, though, we would see the depth of relationships possible in church, and we would lose interest in practicing our faith alone. "And let us consider how to provoke one another to love and good deeds, not neglecting to meet together, as is the habit of some, but encouraging one another, and all the more as you see the Day approaching" (Hebrews 10:24–25).

I want my daughter to see the Church in all its beauty too. (Notice the difference between capital C Church and lowercase church—we are so much more than the denomination or tradition we know best!) I show her this by introducing her to its width and depth. She often visits other churches with me; we've attended services with Quakers, Methodists, Baptists, Church of God, Catholics, Orthodox, and Episcopalians. This always leads to rich discussions about what felt familiar, what might be useful to implement in our own family or in our local church, and things we can appreciate about a particular tradition. There's a phrase that commonly concludes prayer in some of our churches. The *Gloria Patri* says: "Glory be to the Father, and to the Son, and to the Holy Ghost; As it was in the beginning, is now, and ever shall be: world without end." No matter how shaky things seem, you, my daughter, and myself as Christians have an established place in this glorious truth.

When I hear of people who are deconstructing their faith, I encourage them to go wider. Church is about so much more than the one or two ways you've experienced it. Interacting with Christians from other traditions, ethnicities, places around the world, etcetera helps us get to know one another. It reminds us Christianity isn't American, and its roots weren't established in the sixteenth century at the height of the European Reformation. Here's what it's really all about: getting to know more of Christ and getting to know one another. Then, when disaster strikes, we'll have somewhere, and someone, or someones, to turn to.

CHAPTER 22

A Priest at a Funeral

I begin each day with holy Mass, receiving Jesus hidden under the appearance of a simple piece of bread. Then I go out into the streets, and I find the same Jesus hidden in the dying destitute, the AIDS patients, lepers, the abandoned children, the hungry, and the homeless. It's the same Jesus.

— Mother Teresa

My neighbor's dad passed away recently. She had seen him only a few weeks prior, even though they lived several states away from one another, so that was good. We received information about funeral arrangements, and I read the service would be a Catholic Mass at St. Mary's in downtown Grand Rapids. Of course, I wanted to attend the service to support my grieving friend. If I'm totally honest, I was also excited to have an opportunity to attend Mass at such a regal church as well.

I knew the church because every time we drive by it on the highway, my daughter points out the window at the high steeple. "Look at that church," she says.

Another neighbor went with me to the service. She grew up Catholic, so I had an increased comfort level knowing I'd be sitting with someone who knew what she was doing. I've gotten better at recognizing where we are in their liturgy, but still stumble.

Envision the church with me. There's at least one in almost every town, I suspect. A vast sanctuary with high ceilings. Rows of wooden pews with kneelers. The stations of the cross hung around the perimeter. Enough stained glass to make one swoon. It didn't

134

seem appropriate to gawk, but that's exactly what I wanted to do. It seemed equally inappropriate to be excited for the service to begin. I mentioned this to my grieving neighbor later, and as she knows me well, she understood. "Dad had always wanted a Mass at St. Mary's," she said. What a wonderful way to honor him.

No one at the service appeared to be members of this parish. Actually, most of the family and friends in attendance were not Catholic, or not practicing Catholics. The priest had not met the deceased, but had learned of and graciously mentioned the affinity my friend's dad had for windmill cookies. If you're from Dutch country in southwest Michigan and perhaps elsewhere too, you know.

The service included elements I hadn't encountered before, such as swinging the thurible over the body, spreading the incense smoke over it. The casket was closed and covered it with a white cloth, signifying the individual had been clothed in baptism. A soloist sang "Ave Maria," traditional at Catholic funerals. One of the granddaughters also sang, filling the sanctuary with a contemporary praise and worship song. God didn't seem to mind.

As I listened to the words of the homily, and observed the priest as he officiated the service, I could see clearly he was meant to represent the shepherding characteristics we find in Jesus. The priest offered comfort to those loved ones and walked them through a sound theology of death. This realization struck me in a way I have not experienced with the pastors of my church traditions. He wasn't only a godly example, teaching us scripture and guiding our discipleship journey. I saw it clearly here, how the priest was intended to represent Jesus Christ, our Great Comforter.

It came time for the Eucharist. I knew it was coming and was already curious how this portion of the service would go, with so many non-Catholics in attendance. Two family members went to a table in the back to get the chalice and paten, the cup and plate used in the rite, walking them up the aisle to the priest. The priest noted that Eucharist was meant for those in communion with the Catholic Church. I don't know how many people went forward to receive the body and blood, because I became hyperfocused on what I was going to do.

I've never taken communion with Catholics, having known for years I couldn't do so. It used to upset me, but I've come to respect the way they understand this sacrament. A few years ago, I talked with a friend who said he always goes forward to receive a blessing from the priest when he attends Mass. Standing before the priest, my friend crosses his arms across his chest to indicate the desire for a blessing rather than the elements of communion. The priest reaches out his hand, often placing it on my friend's forehead, and says something to the effect of, "May God bless you."

Since I had this conversation, and after doing some further reading, I go forward to receive a blessing from the priest every time I attend Mass. It usually takes him by surprise, as it's often me, and the young children who have yet to receive their first communion, asking for a blessing. I've come to treasure this spiritual moment. If there's any unsettledness in my life at that time, a blessing from a priest feels like a divine touch, and that helps. On this funereal Saturday morning, though, I'm seated by someone I've never gone to church with, and I know there are a number of people who aren't going to be receiving communion. I'm going to stick out if I do my standard walking of the aisle.

After considering my options, I did what I do. I stepped out of my pew, into the aisle, went to the back of the line, and waited my turn. When I stood before the priest, I crossed my arms, he put the unleavened wafer back in the tray, and administered a short blessing on my behalf. I returned to my seat, and eventually my racing heartbeat returned to normal.

Later in the day, my grieving neighbor and her sister stopped by my house to drop something off. We discussed Mass, and agreed it was a good and proper farewell. They asked me about going forward for a blessing, not knowing that was an option. Sometimes the priest will mention it, but this priest had not. We wondered how many people would have gone up if they had known, and what additional comfort doing so might have offered.

To stand before this representative of Christ and hear a word of blessing. Neither of these women are practicing Catholics anymore. They wouldn't have dreamed of receiving communion, although they were baptized in the church. However, they wished they had received a blessing.

I thought back to the priest, and how clearly he exhibited the characteristics of a shepherd among the mourners at the funeral. As members of the body, we too are representatives of Christ. Something about these times of grief reminds us of our need for spiritual blessing as we're trying our best to figure life out.

■ ■ ■

When our daughter was about three or four, escalators frightened her. More than once, I either picked her up to go on the escalator, or we turned around and went to the stairs or an elevator instead. She was with her dad and me at the mall one day, and we were going down to the lower level. We got to the escalator ahead of her, turning to see if she'd join us. We could see her reach her tiny foot out to take a step onto the escalator, but then she'd pull it back. She did this a few times and then successfully put both feet on an escalator step. It's a good thing because looking back, I'm not sure we had a game plan for the alternative.

She was elated at her accomplishment. Looking all around her, she noticed another couple getting on the escalator behind us. "Good job, guys," she told them.

In Peter's first letter, addressed to God's chosen people, he writes: "But you are a chosen race, a royal priesthood, a holy nation, God's own people, in order that you may proclaim the mighty acts of him who called you out of darkness into his marvelous light" (1 Peter 2:9).

Royal priests, you and me. Baptism robes and crowns. We too can show others the goodness of God. Think of the humble position a person takes when they stand before a priest, asking for a blessing. Is a blessing anything other than another way of saying,

"Good job, guys?" What if we approached one another that way? I could stand to learn a lot about receiving blessings from others, because I'd much rather be giving them. What if we all worked harder to see those around us, those so unsteady on their feet, arms crossed in front of their chest, asking if anyone will give them a blessing? Maybe it's a meal, or a financial contribution, or an invite to join you at home or at church, or a kind word, or a healing touch. Go and bless one another in Jesus's name.

CHAPTER 23

The House of the Lord

In the same way the Church exists for nothing else but to draw men into Christ, to make them little Christs. If they are not doing that, all the cathedrals, clergy, missions, sermons, even the Bible itself, are simply a waste of time.

—C. S. Lewis, *Mere Christianity*

Maybe you consider yourself a Christian, but you don't feel as if you fit in any one church anymore. Or you can't do church right now at all. Or maybe you feel like Jesus calls to you from time to time, and you wonder what it would be like here in the body of Christ. Let me walk you through what God is teaching me about church.

There are any number of reasons Christians choose a particular church, a particular tradition or not. Most of us don't choose local churches based on an exhaustive look at the theological nuances. In my twenties, I regularly attended a Presbyterian church for a while, not because I'd decided they lined up perfectly with my belief system but because they had the most active singles group in town at the time.

For some, they are in communion with the church tradition of their family of origin. Others are still part of the same historic tradition but have moved laterally across progressive and conservative lines within a particular branch. Maybe someone prefers a formal liturgy, while others enjoy a contemporary style of worship.

Those of us who have found a local congregation, we mostly just want to feel at home. I'm at home in a worship service among evangelical Protestants, because that's how I grew up. Overall, I like how Sunday mornings make me feel, prepared to face the week ahead. I like a dynamic pastor. I enjoy taking sermon notes.

I have friends who grew up Catholic but aren't practicing their faith in a church. In most instances, they have seen hypocrisy (insider's scoop, it's everywhere) and they stopped going long enough that it's simply no longer a part of their weekly routine. Yet, when I've gone to Mass with them, they still remember most of it. Words memorized long ago come unbidden to their lips. We know about worship at a deep soul level. Sometimes these friends acknowledge missing church, and they might try going to an evangelical service instead, or something in between like a Lutheran or Anglican service. Nothing feels quite right, though. They're left wandering, and while I believe they are Christians, they're missing out on the fellowship and ministry one can only find among a local body of believers.

As I write publicly about exploring other traditions, I'm often asked why I haven't switched to a different church tradition. My answer to this has changed some over time. It's not because I keep a running list of what traditions are right, and which ones are wrong. It's not because I wouldn't feel comfortable in a new tradition, because given enough time, I'm sure the ways they worship would feel natural to me as well. I haven't joined another congregation or denomination other than my own because God has not asked me to. I'm committed to a local church who recognizes me as family. Together, we go deeper in our faith, and wider when, together, we learn about church history, the liturgical calendar, and other spiritual practices. We serve our community and one another. My pastors are mentors of mine. Most days, I love my church.

■ ■ ■

There are as many reasons why people don't attend church. Here are some I've heard: it's my only day off from work and other activities; I never felt connected at my last church; I've been hurt by the church; my kids have sports or other extracurriculars during the worship time; you can be a Christian and not go to church; I experience God more in nature than I do in a building. We all have seasons of our lives, and some of these might apply to you for a time. Eventually, though, God wants you serving him in a local church. I hope you've internalized in these pages that churches and spiritual groups come in all shapes and sizes. If you're unable to do church as you have in the past, ask God to reshape your idea of church, to heal those parts that are unwilling to try again, to show you the beauty of finding Christ in community again. A local body of believers can be a big help when things go shaky.

Having said all that, Sunday mornings can be hard for me sometimes. I always get this sense there's more worship to be had, and we're missing out on it. Liturgy. It's even a silky-sounding word, and the Orthodox add "divine" to it. I'd like to have a reader come up on Sunday morning and read the day's scripture passage before we hear the sermon. I'd like to recite a historic creed every time we gather, because we could always use reminding that there are foundational truths we believe and it brings us into an everlasting communion of the saints. Oh, I'd like to sing a hymn most Sundays. Communion every week, please. Maybe read a psalm or two. Not only would it do us all good to collectively praise, lament, and express our misgivings, it would teach the people of God how to use these words of scripture at home in their own prayer life. We could better understand, we don't have to rely entirely on our own words when talking to God, and our prayer life will be the better for it. Often, we hear people say prayer is "talking to God." We could learn together. Prayer should be more of a conversation, with us doing less talking and more listening. Over the years there have been people I wouldn't naturally befriend, and while I know this can actually make church really beautiful if we move beyond our natural tendencies into holy fellowship, that doesn't always make it easy. Some opportunities for growth can only be found by serving in a local church.

I long for what I call "worship fusion," pulling from the rich tradition of liturgy we find throughout Christendom, celebrating our collective heritage, but adding contemporary touches as well. A praise and worship song in Catholic Mass. A Methodist hymn in a Lutheran hymnbook. A prayer of confession from the BCP read aloud at a nondenominational church. I shouldn't have to leave my church to do other liturgical things.

What I sense I'm missing at my local church, I've found to a certain degree online. I'd encourage you to consider all the ways this might be true for you too. I regularly have conversations about things like church and scripture and theology on social media platforms. What a gift to know a huge variety of brothers and sisters in Christ online. It's a constant reminder that Church is bigger than my local, Midwestern Protestant experience.

When our local churches stopped meeting due to health concerns surrounding Covid-19, many of us found ourselves evaluating whether our current church experience left a gap in our lives or not. Further, some of us realized we didn't miss church at all. As a society, we'd be wise to explore these discoveries in our homes and communities. These might be hard conversations, but refining ones.

One of the gifts we received from the months spent quarantining is a reformation of sorts in how we interact with the Church. When we could not gather and recite the historic creeds together, we could say them from our own living rooms and find a renewed sense of who we join together with in saying these "I believe" statements.

While quarantined, my own church offered services online each week. We held our Bible studies via Zoom. There was even a session of Zoom meetings where we could chat with the pastors. All of this was new to us, but we learned how to do it effectively. For a few weeks it felt novel and exciting, and it felt like a good kind of cheating to sit in my pajamas on my couch for church. But the new wore off quickly, and I longed to be at church on Sunday mornings.

Regardless of where you land on this broad spectrum of church attendance, the church has plenty of new terrain to explore in the digital and online worlds. Based on what I've experienced so far, the virtual opportunities will add richness to our faith lives if we prayerfully discern how to incorporate them into our regular practices.

I've made virtual friends from around the world and they kept me company during the earliest days of the pandemic. In many ways, the bottom was dropping out around me, but I had the fellowship of other Christians to sustain me. People began to share about Zoom opportunities for Bible studies and worship services and book clubs. I have friends who worshiped with three or four churches each Sunday. I was able to watch Catholic Mass in England, Lenten services in Scotland, a Lessons and Carols service from Kansas City, Missouri, and via YouTube, a Taizé video (a repetitive singing of prayer chants that focus on simple phrases, often from Scripture, sung in canon, with the repetitiveness of the music and prayer creating a meditative prayer experience). Plus countless sermons, podcasts, and speaking appearances. If you're looking to connect with Christians who worship differently than you do, or if you need to stay home from church for a time, pick up your electronic device. This is something I'll continue moving forward. These virtual experiences are another way to ground ourselves in our faith.

But nothing gives us a landing place like our local church does. You can find a size, a worship style, and ministry focus that (mostly) fits you. When you feel God prompting you to try church again, I'm always going to be cheering you on. No hurry though.

■ ■ ■

We have a new associate pastor at church, and I've been slowly getting to know him better. He's a cradle Reformer, which means born and raised in the Reformed tradition. People who have stayed in one tradition always fascinate me. No one stays where they are because it's been a perfect experience. Church will not ever be, for anyone, a perfect experience. He's made decisions along the way to stay affiliated with this particular tradition.

I don't know how much Pastor Scott knows about my work. When we talk, it's usually church business or sports. He must know some, though, because sometimes in our meetings, he'll mention something that lets me know he's heard of my passion for all things Church. At the end of one meeting he said, "You know, there are Reformed churches that are highly liturgical." My ears perked up. He said a few miles south of us, in Kalamazoo, there's a Reformed congregation that's much more formal in their worship. Second Reformed Church, I don't know when exactly, but I'm going to stop in some Sunday morning for a visit. I can't wait to meet you.

In my first book, *Not All Who Wander (Spiritually) Are Lost*, I had this to say about my church: "North Point is my church family. What they offer me in the way of spiritual practices and liturgical worship isn't enough. One church can't offer me enough. Not this side of glory."

My pastor's words inform me the Reformed tradition is a big one. Many of our traditions are huge in number. The Southern Baptist Convention, for example, is America's largest Protestant denomination, with more than fifty thousand cooperating churches and church-type missions worldwide. They maintain local church autonomy under a larger umbrella. If you've had one experience in a particular church tradition, know you have not experienced all it has to offer. I know Southern Baptist churches that recite the Apostles' Creed, read psalms liturgically during Sunday morning service, and follow the church calendar. The churches of my childhood did none of these things.

We like to make blanket statements. Baptists all vote Republican. Methodists only keep their pastors for a few years. Episcopalians pride themselves on having women in leadership roles. Saying things like this isn't true or helpful. Blanket statements don't help us get to know one another or leave us open to finding Christ at work among us. It needs to stop; our witness depends on it. "That they may all be one. As you, Father, are in me and I am in you, may they also be in us, *so that the world may believe that you have sent me*" (John 17:21, italics mine).

I'm pleased to discover the Reformed tradition gives me room to wander. They've been in the business of church reform for about five hundred years. They also give me a place in church history and a church from which to serve my community. I wish more of our churches encouraged us to view Christianity as a consecrated mosaic. Get to know the body of Christ. She's exquisite to behold.

CHAPTER 24

Heart of Worship

Without grace, the Christian liturgy is hollow, and fruitful participation in it is impossible. The liturgy, like everything good in life, is an instance of grace.

—Patrick Malloy, *Celebrating the Eucharist*

Liturgy will carry you. Those seasons when you're not sure what you believe. Those moments when you're struggling with the church, or your family, or a job, or any number of other things. Those times when you're in between decisions and the way forward is not yet clear. Those days when your heart longs for the sacred. Those times when you've lived your week among chaos, and you need to be reminded of what is true.

God longs for authentic worship; sometimes this includes big feelings, and sometimes it doesn't. "You profane me when you say, 'Worship is not important, and what we bring to worship is of no account' and when you say, 'I'm bored—this doesn't do anything for me.' You act so superior, sticking your noses in the air—act superior to *me*, God-of-the-Angel-Armies! And when you do offer something to me, it's a hand-me-down, or broken, or useless. Do you think I'm going to accept it? This is God speaking to you!" (Malachi 1:12–13, MSG). The heart of worship isn't about conjuring up our emotions, but about an ongoing commitment to glorify God and participate fully in a local body of believers.

One of my biggest hurdles to pure worship is pride. It gets in the way of letting liturgy shape me. I remember one Sunday I stood in my church, singing a praise and worship song, and found myself wondering what an Orthodox church might be doing at that moment in their service. Maybe something more sophisticated. Likely a chant from the second century. Our candles were battery-operated. As you can imagine, my worship was rendered ineffective. Unacceptable to God, and nothing but a distraction to me.

The truth is, all churches have a liturgical rhythm, some more formal than others. The rhythm of a more formal, eucharistic liturgy references a hefty amount of scripture throughout, and ties one to the universal church that is thousands of years old. Contemporary services have a form of liturgy too. In my church, we begin with a welcome and announcements, followed by three songs, the sermon, and close with a song. On the third Sunday, we include communion. Although we don't receive it weekly, even we know what to do when we hear the familiar words, "'The Lord Jesus on the night when he was betrayed . . .'" (1 Corinthians 11:23). Within our liturgical structure, there have been certain songs we sang at the exact time I needed them, and a refreshing spirit washed over me. We have a woman in our praise band who prays meaningful extemporaneous prayers. There might be a point or two in the sermon that seem directed right at me. Some Sundays I don't even need a sermon to get filled up spiritually, as the spirit reminds me of the stories all around the room. Among the people in my church, I see the women who survived breast cancer, the members of the worship team who have had major heart troubles, the family who just adopted a little boy, the widow and widower who are newly-weds, and always the children. God at work in our lives is worship. Liturgy—the words, the actions, the other members of the body—lends itself to right worship.

Liturgy will form you. It carries us into the mystery of God in our lives. Structuring our liturgy around things like a lectionary and scripture brings harmony to God's word and our corporate worship. A proper balance can be struck between word and sacrament. Doing the same things each week removes our need for an emotional high and settles us into a routine of walking with

God, no matter what we're feeling. It can teach us ways to worship together and give us the tools to do so at home as well.

I've worshiped with Gregorian chants, instrumental music, hymns, African spirituals, praise and worship, children's Sunday school songs, full choirs. Poetry—the oft-repeated words of liturgical prayers, songs, the psalms—has a way of seeping into our hearts. The words settle, and before long we find they aren't just for Sunday morning. These lyrical phrases are part of what a church offers. Something to aid in worship in that moment, and in the days, weeks, and years to come. Nothing can calm our soul like poetic words set to music. Can you hear it?

What about the church calendar? Do we need to follow the liturgical calendar, which in its most basic form follows the life, death, and resurrection of Jesus? No, we don't *have* to. Looking back at the contents of this entire book, we won't find many things we have to do. We're attempting to cast off legalism. We want to incorporate regular rhythms to help us stay focused on God. Can you see the subtle but significant shift? As in our daily time with God, when using the church calendar, we're looking to create a spiritual rhythm to our weeks, months, and years as well. I commented to a friend once that I wasn't very good at observing seasons like Lent, meant to mark Jesus's forty days spent in the wilderness. She told me the church calendar is intended to be aspirational, meaning it's full of feast days and fast days, seasons of waiting, of penance, of celebration. More than most of us can accomplish, especially when we're in a group of believers who don't incorporate these seasons into their scheduling. "That's kind of the point," she said. Aspirational. Observing the calendar keeps us growing, keeps us seeking, keeps us humble.

In the few years I've been observing the church calendar, I've noticed an added meaningfulness to my celebrations of Christmas and Easter in particular. Going through seasons like Advent and Lent offers an opportunity for preparation, slowing down the journeys to the manger and the cross, suggesting specific topics of reflection. Advent is recognized as a time of waiting, while Lent focuses on the three spiritual practices Christ mentions in his Sermon on the Mount: fasting, prayer, and almsgiving (Matthew 6:1–18). These seasons have also become times of training in my life. I might find myself waiting on news about a book proposal, for example, and it's not Advent, not December, but I am able to recognize that I'm in a season of waiting. I can think back on what I've learned about waiting during Advent, and apply the things I've learned, claiming hope because I am in Christ, knowing I can trust his timing.

What should our churches look like structurally? They should be spaces that take us by the hand and lead us to worship. Can we see how those who use icons and statues and candles use their senses to aid in worship? Is it possible to transform a space used for something else during the week into a worshipful space? Yes, I worshipped in a place like this for several years.

Personally, I am partial to a building that looks like a church. It lends itself to a spiritual settling, where I can immediately set my heart to worship. There are some who have negative responses to the lofty structures that have been built in homage to Christianity through the years. All that money and resources on what is seemingly just a building. As a friend pointed out to me, these places of sacred beauty are for everyone. Anyone can walk in these doors and pray, soaking up the reverent atmosphere. You might know people who feel older churches can seem stuffy, and modern church buildings often try to create a more relaxed, homey atmosphere for these people. I can easily debate the various sides. God and I have done some work on my pride in this area as well.

Here's where my friend Nancy goes to church: "[My church] isn't really a church. It's St. Vincent de Paul pantry. It's way too small, has no pews, just chairs, and no song books. It's always crowded with old and not so old people, children and babies. Black, white, and more. We pray together, laugh together, and share the burdens of others. We help with their spiritual hunger, as well as their physical hunger. We help to keep their lights on and keep their babies warm. We lift up those in need, encourage those who are doing what they can, and look for Jesus in each of them. We pray that they see Jesus in us. It doesn't get any better."

I want to go to Nancy's church. Church is made up of people. Every one of them has a story.

How I long for you to find a healthy church too. So I can visit, of course. I'd encourage you to take a moment and make a list of what you think a healthy church should offer. You can think through the things we've mentioned here: worship music, a place to gather, people who pray and read scripture together, ministry to the community, and an overall rhythm that helps us center on the life of Christ. Feel free to add more items.

I like the Bible stories of Jesus practicing his faith. My New Testament has notes throughout, observing those times when Jesus went to a Jewish festival, practiced the Sabbath, referenced a law they were instructed to keep. Religion gets a bad name sometimes. At its core, our religion is believing in God and worshipping him. Together, we do that in church. We bring our flaws and our weaknesses, attempt to dress them up enough to be seen in public, and stumble to the cross together. Sometimes it helps me tremendously to strip a concept free from everything I thought it was and look at it down at its core. When I gather with my brothers and sisters, my church family, in our house of worship, I experience God's grace and mercy with them. This happens when I visit too, because I'm still among the body of Christ. With a right heart, fashioned so by the work God and I have done in the days prior, I'm reminded of the hope we profess. Nothing else has given me the connection to Christ and to others that church has. And I mean church in its most basic definition, alongside our historical understanding. In the Greek, *ekklesia*, or simply "called out by God." This is church.

PART V

ASSURANCE

CHAPTER 25

Gifts of the Church

Christianity has suffered more casualties from faux faith than from honest doubt.

—Brian Zahnd, *When Everything's on Fire*

n *Always a Guest: Speaking of Faith Far from Home,* Barbara Brown Taylor shares a collection of stories and sermons from those times when she is invited to be a guest at a church, a university, or a conference. She writes, "The first gift of guest preaching was the loosening of denominational bonds. I learned how to wait for the Spirit to move in a Pentecostal church, even if it meant the sermon started late and ended even later. I learned that thirty minutes was about right for Baptists and too long for Lutherans. I spoke in gymnasiums, under tents, on stages, and in cafeterias, without any familiar furniture or forms or worship. The disorientation was dazzling. None of my Episcopal lingo worked. I had to reach for language that lived closer to the heart of common Christian experience."

Dazzling. Perhaps because as a guest preacher, the congregation is always new, a beginning of sorts. You haven't walked together in community with these people. You don't know who you like and who you might rather avoid. If someone reacts negatively to your sermon, chances are they'll e-mail their regular pastor, not you, to register their complaint. I'm that new person in a congregation a lot because I frequently visit other churches. It does offer a different look at things. It's the end of Taylor's quote that gripped me: "Language that lived closer to the heart of common Christian experience."

In these final chapters, we're going to look at what I call gifts of the Church. Things we experience in community as the beat of our collective religious hearts. You don't have to be well versed in church speak to recognize the devotion found in practicing these gifts. All you need to know is what it's like to commit your life to something or someone. You have to love that thing you're committed to so much you miss it terribly when you're away from it. When we practice these gifts regularly, with right intent toward one another, it's as if heaven opens up to show us a glimpse of all we have to look forward to.

■ ■ ■

You've no doubt heard stories of people on their deathbed. Often, dementia has taken away large parts of their identity, making it difficult for loved ones who only see a shell of the person they knew, grieving the loss even before they've died. Much of what the afflicted person says appears to be nonsense. That is until common prayers or creeds, those words they memorized perhaps as children, and repeated in liturgy hundreds of times by this point in their life, come to mind. Doctors call it muscle memory. That area of the brain that stores procedural memory is slower to be affected by deterioration from disease. After praying or singing these words for years, it doesn't require as much mental fortitude to recall them. What a gift to have the words on their lips in those final days be a prayer to God, such as this phrase from a eucharistic prayer: "It is indeed good, right, and salutary that we should at all times and in all places offer thanks and praise to You, O Lord, Holy Father, through Christ our Lord."

Maybe you're still considering what you believe about Church and the communion of saints overall. It could be you used to fit in perfectly among a certain church or tradition, but your paths have diverged. Creeds and catechisms were created as tools to guide this journey and to help shape our questions. To point us to Christ's soild ground, again and again. We live in a day when the various tools used throughout church history are available at our fingertips—not just the creeds and catechism questions and answers but forms of prayer and liturgical practice that connect us to people of faith down through the centuries. Remember, we don't have to examine every single word or every single document to identify what's right. We want to know God better. The body of Christ, capital C Church, can help with that. I know this because it is helping me.

CHAPTER 26

Breaking Bread

We come to see that God IS communion and that kinship is
God's only thirst.

—Gregory Boyle, *The Whole Language*

The sacraments are rites in the church meant to be visible forms of
grace. Protestant Christians generally "recognize," or practice,
two: baptism and communion. Catholics have seven sacraments:
baptism, confirmation, Eucharist, penance, anointing of the sick,
matrimony, and holy orders. The Orthodox don't categorize these
sacred acts in quite the same way, but instead call them Mysteries.

When the ground under our feet gets especially shaky, we consider spiritual things more than we might have in some time. For
some, especially if the church is part of the shake-up, they need to
step away for a time, even if that means missing a regular issuance
of the sacraments. If this is you, know you remain part of the body
of Christ. You are still one of us. I take such comfort in the promise
Paul writes in a letter to his son in the faith, Timothy. "The saying
is sure: If we have died with him, we will also live with him; if we
endure, we will also reign with him; if we deny him, he will also
deny us; if we are faithless, he remains faithful—for he cannot deny
himself" (2 Timothy 2:11–13).

For others, they simply can't imagine not being among the body
of Christ. Things like the sacraments, comforting words of blessing

from a priest, a coming together to confess what we believe, helps to put us back on solid footing.

The stories in this chapter and the next are about the two sacraments I know best, and the grace I've seen exhibited in them. The longer I'm walking The Way, the more I appreciate these tangible signs of grace. They point us home.

■ ■ ■

I once attended a Russian Orthodox Divine Liturgy with my mother and young daughter. I'm not sure how I talk people into participating in these new ways of doing church with me, but it was nice to have them along. The first person we met at the liturgy happened to be a deacon's wife, who whispered to us throughout the service, explaining some of what was going on. Bless her. As a congregation, we chanted while the priest and deacons went to the altar table (some might call it the proskomedia table), to prepare the bread and wine. Protestants cannot participate in the Eucharist in Orthodox worship because we are not in full unity. I enjoyed observing, though. During this time, the children began forming a single-file line. Moms with young children, even infants, lined up as well. The deacon's wife told me children would receive Eucharist first. In the Orthodox church, as with some other traditions, an infant receives the Eucharist upon being baptized.

A loaf of bread had been baked for the service that morning. A portion of it was cut and consecrated. The remaining loaf was broken up into pieces and put on a plate off to the side of the communion line. The consecrated bread was placed in the cup of wine. Each person who received Eucharist from the priest was served a morsel of the bread, soaked in the wine, via a spoon. The deacons held a linen cloth under the cup to ensure nothing was spilled. I enjoyed watching the children receive Eucharist, especially those tiny babies in their mothers' arms. A few men helped Miriam, an elderly woman I had met that morning, take the steps to the altar area so she could receive the bread and wine as well. Chanting continued the entire time.

The portion of the bread on the side table is called antidoron (ordinary leavened bread, which is blessed but not consecrated and distributed in Eastern Orthodox churches that use the Byzantine Rite). After people received communion, they'd stop at the table and eat a piece of this bread, which spoke of fellowship, breaking bread together, to me. I had read that if someone wanted to, they could take a piece of this bread and offer it in fellowship to non-Orthodox people in attendance.

No one offered me that bread, but at the end of the service (two hours and fifteen minutes after it began), the priest, the deacons, and the maybe-bishop formed a receiving line. The priest held the plate of antidoron and one of the deacons held the blessing cross. One by one, people went to this line, reached down to kiss the cross, and ate another piece of bread. I wasn't positive, but I was pretty sure this part included me. I looked to my mom, who mouthed, "nope," then to my daughter, who rolled her eyes because she was d-o-n-e, and decided to get in line by myself. I cannot kiss the cross, you guys. I love Jesus. Oh goodness, yes. So, I did as I've done previously at a Good Friday service with the Catholics. I reached down with my fingers, and reverently touched the cross. Lord, know my heart. I took my bread from the priest and returned to my spot on the floor. It wasn't quite communion, but it felt like a tremendously kind gesture.

I have since received this kindness another time. Have you ever met someone who becomes such a dear friend that you wish you could more vividly remember when and how you met in the first place, but you had no way of knowing at the time you were meeting someone who would have such a profound effect on your life? That's how I feel about Phoebe, whom I've mentioned previously in this book. She also writes about her faith. Her husband is her priest. We've written a few blog posts for one another over the years. Phoebe never makes me feel awkward for asking dumb questions (and I have a lot of them). I value her friendship, my sister in Christ.

My family went on vacation one summer, and as it turned out, our destination was only a few hours from Phoebe's home. We agreed to meet at a restaurant halfway between where we were and her city. I brought my daughter and Phoebe arrived with her three children and husband, the priest, in tow. We offered quick introductions and then her husband, who wore his full vestment, reached into a pocket and retrieved a morsel of bread. The family had attended vespers before coming to see me. This bread came from the unconsecrated portion of the freshly baked loaf. Her family had fasted before receiving the Eucharist, as is their practice, then raced to the restaurant for our lunch. They were starving. Yet, they took the time to bring me a piece of that bread, and before we ate a meal together, I ate it.

My Orthodox brothers and sisters and I don't take the Eucharist together. It saddens me, although I know they have their reasons and they seek holiness and truth in the carrying out of this decision. Perhaps that's why the morsel of unconsecrated bread means so much. In this simple act of charity, it is as if they say, we know you are also seeking Christ.

"While they were eating, Jesus took a loaf of bread, and after blessing it he broke it, gave it to the disciples, and said, 'Take, eat; this is my body.' Then he took a cup, and after giving thanks he gave it to them, saying, 'Drink from it, all of you; for this is my blood of the covenant, which is poured out for many for the forgiveness of sins'" (Matthew 26:26–28).

I grew up taking the Lord's Supper once a quarter. I didn't think much of it. While the moment felt special, it wasn't anything I missed the other eleven (or so) Sundays in between. Later, I would read about Christians who took communion more frequently, even daily.

Some Christians situate their sanctuaries around the communion table, making it the center of everything. Many Christian churches house the consecrated elements in a box called the tabernacle ("dwelling place"), partially as a reminder of the words we read in the gospel of John, "And the Word became flesh and lived among us, and we have seen his glory, the glory as of a father's only

son, full of grace and truth" (John 1:14). If we home in on the word
"lived" (other translations use "dwelt") in that verse, in the Greek it
is literally "to pitch his tent," much like the tabernacle the Israelites
built in the wilderness, which God filled with his glory. Every time
Catholics, Episcopalians, and others gather for the Eucharist, the
reminder is right there: Christ tabernacled among us.

I asked a pastor once why some Protestants don't take communion every week. My local church now takes it every third Sunday (I'm progressing). Do you ever have conversations where you
hear an answer and at the time you can't think of a good response?
He told me he'd heard it was not a good idea to offer communion
every week because it would lose its meaning due to regularity. I
nodded, knowing full well I'd think about that statement for some
time. And I have now thought about that statement for some time.
If you'll allow me the space, I'd like to give it a response.

Hogwash. Malarky. No way, no how.

When we found ourselves socially distanced from our church
family, the observances of communion and baptism came to a halt
for a time. After a few months, our pastors decided we would take
communion together, from a distance. As evangelicals who didn't
use specially consecrated bread, or a specific brand of wine, we
were uniquely equipped to do this. After all the reading, all the
church visits, all the hours thinking about communion, I was more
than ready to serve it in my home. We made hot rolls, full of leaven.
My husband had a fresh batch of mead (honey wine) he'd recently
bottled. I placed these elements in some pottery that is meaningful
to us because it was formed by the hands of a family member. On
a prerecorded video, our pastor led us through the various parts of
the service. We watched his family receive their portion. One by
one, we served one another the warm bread, the sweet wine. This.
This too was communion.

I've decided somewhere along this journey to leave the arguing
to the experts. At my church, when I take that morsel of pita bread
and dip it in the bowl of grape juice, what happens? It's more than
a symbol. I don't sense Jesus living in me any more than his spirit

already does. I can only tell you it's profoundly significant, dripping with meaning. Lord, forgive us for the times we've made it anything less than holy. I'd take communion every day if I could.

■ ■ ■

Margaret Feinberg travels to various locales where she learns more about the food and seasonings we read about in scripture. She tells some of her stories in the book *Taste and See*. In the section on bread, Feinberg went to Israel to learn about the ingredients they use, baking methods, that sort of thing. She writes:

> One of my most regrettable moments in Israel involved our daily bread. Ido's family and staff and I shared many meals together. We grew close fast, and I transformed from new found friend to long-lost cousin.
>
> Every meal featured all the bread anyone could eat. The meals before Passover included enormous focaccia drizzled with olive oil and dotted with fresh garlic. Like mine, most people's eyes were bigger than their bellies. Long after the plates were cleared, huge slabs of the uneaten bread remained on the tables.
>
> In a desire to help, I cleaned and tossed the leftovers for the first few days. Then I became curious, for it seemed as if the bread had been left purposely to linger on the tables.
>
> "Because it's holy," Mama Vered explained. "We offer it to the poor, and if they do not take it, we feed the birds and fish, but we never throw bread away."

Bread has a long history of being holy. Who am I to question the meaning of it for another individual, my brother and sister in Christ, to put the body and blood of our Lord on their lips? May we echo what Mama Vered knew to be true even with the bread of every day: it's holy. Take, eat.

CHAPTER 27

Holy Water

The heavens were opened to show us that our baptism will
open the heavens for us. God is made accessible to us. We
can know the Unknowable. We can be changed.

—John Chrysostom

n her gorgeous book *Birthing Hope*, Rachel Marie Stone describes the
baptistery in her father's church growing up:

> The baptistery was under the floor where my father stood
> to preach on ordinary Sundays. . . . The floor beneath the
> pulpit was flimsy. During a boring sermon I amused myself
> by it giving way as a dunk-the-clown carnival gag, acciden-
> tally rebaptizing my very surprised dad. I used to help him
> fill it, and sometimes longed to take a dip in it myself, after I'd
> learned to swim, but though we Baptists didn't believe in such
> a thing as holy water, to swim in a baptistery would've consti-
> tuted some kind of sacrilege nonetheless.

The sacraments captivate us from an early age. I witnessed this
with my own daughter one summer when she was around the age
of five, and I saw her at the birdbath, administering the rite of baptism to a mama cat's kittens.

At our church, our children aren't in the sanctuary when we
serve communion. They're already in their classrooms, and a few

times over the years, while teaching, I've shown them the platters we use to serve the bread and the juice. We talk about remembering Jesus in this way, preparing them for receiving communion themselves someday.

They are in the sanctuary to witness baptisms. In our church, we offer both infant baptisms and believer baptisms, which I feel is giving our children a good opportunity for learning how to honor the various ways churches understand the waters of baptism. What I hope they'll take away from the observance of these sacraments lines up more with the Orthodox understanding. During these visible acts of grace, participated in as a church, the veil between daily life and spirituality seems to thin. Men and women over the years have tried to describe what is happening in high-dollar church words. When I learned the Orthodox call them Sacred Mysteries, this was good enough for me. God's ways are bigger than our ways, and God alone knows what great and mighty works occur when the baptismal waters are stirred, when we ingest his body and blood. Is it any wonder these acts move many of us to tears?

There's a phrase I've often heard Christians use—remember your baptism. Now, I was seven when I was baptized, so I have actual memories of this special day. My family attended a country church at the time, so we'd go into town, using the baptismal at First Baptist Church on Sunday afternoons, when we had people to baptize. I can see the pews, the sanctuary well lit with natural light from the many windows. The baptismal tub placed above the choir loft, which actually made an excellent hide-and-seek location in the days of my youth, when we'd have lock-ins at the church.

"Remember your baptism" means so much more than a literal interpretation, though. That's the sacred value of the sacraments. We could make a whole list of what ceremonial acts like baptism and communion invite us to remember.

Remember whose you are. Remember you were bought at a price. Remember he who saved you will never let you go. Remember you're part of something bigger, so much bigger, than yourself. Remember you are inseparable from your brothers and sisters in

Christ. Take a moment and insert your own remember statements, because these I mention are only a few. Oh, the glorious riches of being in Christ Jesus.

These three words, remember your baptism, have impacted me. I hear the phrase whispered often to my spirit in church services I attend. But also at other times. Water, in its purest form, is life-giving. We cannot survive without good, clean water. When my family has supported missions around the world, drinkable water is one of the greatest gifts we've had to offer. I live by Lake Michigan, where you stand on one shoreline and cannot see the other. How often my mind has turned to God when I observe the vastness of this body of water.

In the opening words of scripture, we read: "When God began to create heaven and earth, and the earth then was welter and waste and darkness over the deep and God's breath hovering over the waters" (Genesis 1:1–2, Alter). Then, God called forth light.

Remember your baptism. For our lives too, before Jesus, were welter and waste and darkness. God's breath hovered. He brought you into the light. He created life in the beginning. He's still creating new life in you and me.

CHAPTER 28

Room for Doubt

Faith is not the suppression of doubt. It is the overcoming
of doubt, and you overcome doubt by going through it.

—Thomas Merton

One biblical picture of baptism is when we baptize an entire family (see Acts 16:15, 33; 18:8; 1 Corinthians 1:16). The up-to-
then-unbaptized parents and older children are immersed
in a believer's baptism, while the younger members of the family
are baptized into God's covenant relationship with believers, with
the family and members of the church expressing their confidence
in God to draw the children unto himself. From there, the family
become disciples together, growing in their faith and serving God
through the local church. In my reformed tradition, I've seen this
spiritual transformation happen among families. What a privilege
to partner in the discipling process, as an entire family unit turns to
Jesus together.

I am a product of this kind of baptism. Sort of. Although my
mom grew up in the church, she had a personal salvation experience as a young mom. While pregnant with me, she was baptized.
Although my dad did not share in the experiences, my brothers and
I watched Mom mature in her faith. We saw her develop a rhythm
that included many of the spiritual practices we've discussed in this
book. Although we were not baptized as infants, my brothers and
I accepted God's invitation for ourselves, and we too became disciples. As I look at our collective life experiences, I see specific times

when we held our faith before us, examining it. Through divorces, miscarriages, lost jobs, new homes in faraway cities, health scares, raising children, and living too far away from one another, we have asked hard questions of God. In the darkest nights of my family, I have whispered, "Are you good?" or "Have you left me all alone in this?" Sometimes he gives me clear answers. When he doesn't, we're still spending time together in the asking. God is okay with our doubts too. In fact, I'd say they are encouraged, because God wants to know we trust him enough to appear vulnerable, completely transparent, before him.

A life of faith is not stagnant, sitting around waiting for heaven. It's our lifeline, to God and one another, lived in real time. An ongoing conversation, with God and one another. Some of my most impactful faith conversations happen with my mom and my brothers, because they know me. We share common experiences, and they sang those hymns and learned those same Bible stories that first taught me the ways of faith. Our faith roots go deep, and they're intertwined in such a way that makes us stronger somehow. For me, seeing the unrest in my dad's soul, and the steadfastness in my mom's, showed a clear contrast between a life committed to Jesus Christ and a life that could be set to spinning when things got difficult. My brothers and I share this mutual understanding.

So, as Christians, what do we do when life is unfair? When we cannot settle in our souls exactly what we believe? Flipping to the other side of the same coin, can someone come to me when they have doubts? Am I prepared to walk alongside someone who has very real questions, often borne out of tough circumstances?

"The Doubter's Prayer," a poem by Anne Brontë, addresses these times in life. Here's one stanza:

Oh, help me, God! For thou alone
Canst my distracted soul relieve;
Forsake it not: it is thine own,
Though weak, yet longing to believe.

See why I appreciate poetry? There's a whole essay in these few lines. I've listened to many people express doubts over the years, about the claims Christianity makes regarding the life of Jesus Christ, about the inerrancy of scripture, about how other faiths fit into God's redemptive work. I get it. Looking at my life, I've wondered at God's timing, asked him to intervene in situations with seemingly no response, and I've also questioned whether he would keep loving me if I didn't work hard enough. You can fill in the blanks with your own doubts.

I like that Brontë asks for relief. These doubts can eat at us. They can convince us we should hide them and isolate ourselves from other Christians. From God. They become our focus rather than thinking on what we know to be true.

"Though weak, yet longing to believe."

Living into the fullness of Christ includes our doubts as well as our fears and our disappointments. It has to, because they're a part of us too. What I've learned is to develop a habit of taking them to God. If (when?) they return, bring them to God again. Really, this process never ends.

The author of Hebrews gives us a broad definition of faith, and doubts fit into it: "Now faith is the assurance of things hoped for, the conviction of things not seen" (Hebrews 11:1). Faith. I cannot prove my faith to you. The next time someone stops by my house, I can't take it down from a shelf and show it to them. Standing with other Christians, we can claim things we hope for, and trust God with what we cannot see. If you keep reading in the eleventh chapter of Hebrews, you'll come across an extensive list of names sometimes identified as the Heroes of Faith. You know what? There's not a perfect hero in the mix. Like us, their faith, their trust in God, had to grow over time, and God used circumstances and other people to do it. The ending of this chapter lands a powerful punch: "Yet all these, though they were commended for their faith, did not receive what was promised, since God had provided something better so that they would not, apart from us, be made perfect" (Hebrews 11:39–40).

I need a community that lets me voice my deepest questions about God, and I want it to be local first. In my family, in my small groups, in my church, branching out into those friendships I make online around the world. I want to hold space for your questions too, because this connects us profoundly. It helps tremendously to know we're not alone. You might have walked through a time of doubt similar to the one I'm having and can encourage me along the way. The body of Christ has bruises. There are times we try to amputate one of our limbs, and things like doubt and distrust leave us with a thorn in our flesh, such as Paul had (2 Corinthians 12:7–10). Instead of considering such things weak, I want us to create a faith culture where we realize they're human. Then Church—here's what we can do for one another, and it's one of my favorite things to do—points one another to Jesus again and again.

CHAPTER 29

What We Believe

> A man becomes a Christian, he is not born one.
>
> —Tertullian

want to point us now to things Christians have memorized, often learning the words as children, about the same time I was taking in memory verses and hymn lyrics. These words are certainly taken from scripture, but they are not found there verbatim. Men, along with a scattering of women along the way, have pulled together scriptural truths that form things like creeds, catechisms, and confessions. They're collections about what we believe, and why we believe it. While these were originally intended to be tools of knowledge, we'll see the words also become part of our worship, our prayers. As with so many things, we see a spiritual fluidity here. We might find ourselves reciting a creed in corporate worship, and suddenly tearing up because we realize we have some doubts about a certain line, but those around us, the bigger image of the body of Christ, stand beside us still. We can know it's possible to be carried during this time of questioning and doubt, and next time it may be our turn to do the carrying. After the bottom drops out, we're all still here. Church is built on the surest foundation there is. Each chapter in this section requires a bit of a history lesson but stick with it. There's worship too.

■ ■ ■

There are a few passages in the New Testament that were hymns, prayers, or formal responses recited by early church communities. Many scholars believe the following passage was an early Christian hymn:

> Let the same mind be in you that was in Christ Jesus, who, though he was in the form of God, did not regard equality with God as something to be exploited, but emptied himself, taking the form of a slave, being born in human likeness. And being found in human form, he humbled himself and became obedient to the point of death—even death on a cross. (Philippians 2:5–8)

We find what is possibly one of the earliest creeds (a traditional formula churches would often recite, proclaiming their core beliefs) dating back to circa 30 CE in 1 Corinthians 15:3–7:

> For I handed on to you as of first importance what I in turn had received: that Christ died for our sins in accordance with the scriptures, and that he was buried, and that he was raised on the third day in accordance with the scriptures, and that he appeared to Cephas, then to the twelve. Then he appeared to more than five hundred brothers and sisters at one time, most of whom are still alive, though some have died. Then he appeared to James, then to all the apostles.

In the first three centuries of Christianity, the church did the hard, often fluid work of building an organization. By fluid, I mean identifying common beliefs did not happen in one meeting nor was it presented as specific onetime discussion topics on a meeting agenda. Jesus Christ is the church's foundation, but figurative walls were needed. Church members were still by and large converts, and it became necessary to determine a common belief based on the truths found in scripture. These often came in the form of a statement called a creed ("to believe"), developed at ecumenical councils that brought together church leaders from around the world. Here are two of the most widely used creeds, along with some ideas about how they can help to form the bedrock on which we can stand when we find ourselves in the midst of struggles.

Apostles' Creed

I believe in God, the Father almighty, creator of heaven and earth. I believe in Jesus Christ his only Son, our Lord. He was conceived by power of the Holy Spirit and born of the Virgin Mary. He suffered under Pontius Pilate, was crucified, died, and was buried. He descended to the dead. On the third day he rose again. He ascended into heaven, and is seated at the right hand of the Father. He will come again to judge the living and the dead. I believe in the Holy Spirit, the holy catholic Church, the communion of saints, the forgiveness of sins, the resurrection of the body, and the life everlasting. Amen.

Before we go any further, we should know the word "catholic" is a word that means universal. The proper name, Catholic Church, refers to one church tradition. I'll often mention capital C Church in my writings, to relay this idea of a universal church, which the Apostles' Creed refers to here. Sometimes churches will change the wording of the creed to say universal, or something similar, rather than calling ourselves catholic. It seems a better approach is to explain the historical understanding of the word as presented in the creeds. It's still a very good word.

We're not sure how far back this creed dates. Paul Senz writes: "There is a tradition that the creed comes from the apostles themselves and that each of the Twelve wrote one of the twelve articles on the day of Pentecost after the descent of the Holy Spirit (of course, by this point, St. Matthias had already been chosen to replace Judas Iscariot [Acts 1:12–26])."

The Apostles' Creed likely developed over time out of the baptismal liturgy used in the early churches. Most believers were illiterate, so having short, easily memorable statements helped establish a shared belief system about our triune God.

Nicene Creed

We believe in one God, the Father, the Almighty, maker of heaven and earth, of all that is, seen and unseen.

We believe in one Lord, Jesus Christ, the only Son of God, eternally begotten of the Father, God from God, Light from Light, true God from true God, begotten, not made, of one Being with the Father. Through him all things were made.

For us and for our salvation he came down from heaven: by the power of the Holy Spirit he became incarnate from the Virgin Mary, and was made man.

For our sake he was crucified under Pontius Pilate; he suffered death and was buried. On the third day he rose again in accordance with the Scriptures; he ascended into heaven and is seated at the right hand of the Father. He will come again in glory to judge the living and the dead, and his kingdom will have no end.

We believe in the Holy Spirit, the Lord, the giver of life, who proceeds from the Father and the Son. With the Father and the Son he is worshiped and glorified. He has spoken through the Prophets. We believe in one holy catholic and apostolic Church. We acknowledge one baptism for the forgiveness of sins. We look for the resurrection of the dead, and the life of the world to come. Amen.

This creed comes from the first two ecumenical church councils; in Nicea (325 CE) and in Constantinople (381 CE). Another reason councils convened was to respond to theological controversies. Bishops and other leaders gathered to discern the church's response to heresy. Notice how different this governing approach is compared to the way we hear someone say something about Christianity he or or she doesn't agree with today. How quick we are to call out "heretic." This was a serious accusation considered after months, even years, of questioning the individual who might be determined a heretic. These powerful councils held the authority to determine the fate of the individuals who took a theological stance they deemed unbiblical. Exercising this power, the heretics were often imprisoned or even put to death. Later in church history, one famous church heretic, Galileo, was brought before the Catholic Church's chief inquisitor, Father Vincenzo Maculani da Firenzuola, for believing the earth revolves around the sun, and not the other way around, the position of the Church at that time. In AD 1633, charged with the suspicion of heresy, Galileo agreed to not teach heresy anymore, and spent the rest of his life under house arrest. It would be another three hundred years before the Catholic Church accepted he had been right, and his name was cleared.

Creeds still offer a helpful resource to new believers who are learning to put into words what they believe. We don't have to reinvent the wheel. Use these creeds to outline lessons on what Christians believe. Also, it's been deeply meaningful to me, and others, to realize when Christians make these "I believe" statements, we join countless other believers, in the past, present, and in the future, who are making the same claims. Many believers tell a story of being filled with doubt, maybe even not attending church for a time, then hearing these creeds professed in a worship service. It's powerful to know there are people surrounding you who can believe when you don't fully. Or to hear those words after a time of pain, a time you may have stepped away into the shaky, shaky world, and reciting these words helps you realize there are things you still believe in. Collectively, we cry out: Lord, help our unbelief.

For some of us, in the churches we grew up in, creeds were not mentioned or taught. The closest we got was listening to self-proclaimed ragamuffin (ragged and disreputable) performing artist, Rich Mullins. In 1993, four years before his untimely death, he released a song about what he believed. In this song, simply titled "Creed," he told listeners what he believes makes him, indeed was making him still. He did not make it, and neither did we.

I remember the song, but still had no idea what a creed was. In fact, it would be a decade before I actually knew what Mullins was singing about. A few years beyond that still before I would stand up in full agreement—the words of these creeds make me who I am too. They are making me; before I even knew the words existed, I believed them. What's forming me is the deep understanding that everyone who believes these words, those Christ-followers who wrestle with them in part or in whole, form the body of Christ. We're in this together, even when we fight about that.

You may be asking yourself, "So what?" How important is an orthodox set of beliefs? Why would we need these creeds today? The hard work has already been done, right? You may be in a place where you're not ready to peg down what you believe, or find that the creeds don't seem helpful to your faith—or your doubts—right now.

In *The Creed: What Christians Believe and Why It Matters*, Luke Timothy Johnson writes:

> In a world that celebrates individuality, [millions of Christians] are actually doing something together. In an age that avoids commitment, they pledge themselves to a set of convictions and thereby to each other. In a culture that rewards novelty and creativity, they use words written by others long ago. In a society where accepted wisdom changes by the minute, they claim that some truths are so critical that they must be repeated over and over again. In a throwaway, consumerist world, they accept, preserve, and continue tradition.

In a world where everything seems to further divide us, Christianity should be coming together, rather than creating more shaky ground.

Here's why I appreciate the creeds. The list of what we don't agree on is long, but most Christians can profess the words set forth in the creeds. They are not scripture and they won't ever replace scripture, but they offer common ground. The truths found in these lyrical phrases point us to Christ, the solid rock on which we stand.

One friend mentioned her pastor always asks, "Christian, what do you believe?" before they recite the creed together. Another friend shared about her experience deconstructing her faith and losing a church that closed its doors. Some time later, she attended an Episcopal church, heard the creeds, and it moved her to tears. While much in her life may have felt as though it was slipping away, she knew she still very much believed.

The creeds are rhythmic, following speech patterns –at least in their English translations—that lend themselves to memorization. In that respect, they seem not all that different from the beloved hymns I sang growing up in that small Baptist church. Here's what I have come to realize: anything that helps our minds dwell on God will serve us well. Committing sacred words to memory is a positive thing. I still don't have the Apostles' Creed memorized to the point I can rattle it off quickly, but when I hear the first line or two, my mind goes to these historic words. I'm reminded that working out our faith is what Christians do. While the creeds don't answer every theological point, they give us structure. When I visit other churches—the Methodists, the Anglicans, the Orthodox, the Catholics—I've said the creeds alongside these fellow Christians. It's making me realize that we cannot separate ourselves, no matter how hard we try.

■ ■ ■

It was only a few years ago I set out to commit the Apostles' Creed to memory. It's more difficult for me to memorize things as I get older. I know lines from hymns and Bible verses from my childhood. I can still recite several phone numbers from days gone by (don't ask me any current ones, though). When I set out to memorize the Apostles' Creed, I took pen to paper. It's the best I knew to do. I'd write out one or two lines, carry them around with me, looking at them and saying them out loud for a few weeks. Then I'd add another line from the creed. A few months of working on this process and I can say it fairly well. I'm not a lifer who can recite it in thirty seconds or less, but that is never the point, is it?

I brought the old and the new together in a meaningful way one Sunday afternoon. My olive-green *Baptist Hymnal* was published in 1956. My childhood church gave us a used copy when they switched to newer hymnals. In addition to years of use on Sunday mornings, Sunday evenings, and Wednesday evenings, it has made several moves with me. I still pull it out from time to time and play the songs that have only a few flats and sharps, as my piano playing is limited. After learning the churches of my childhood were noncreedal (a rejection of any creedal statement other than those found in the Bible), I was curious. I flipped through the pages of my hymnal. "Holy, Holy, Holy" was there on page 1, as it should be. I smiled, recalling the story about the controversy that arose upon moving it from that opening page slot in the 2008 hymnal. After the hymns, I noted several pages of responsive readings, which I do recall using from time to time. The final pages were indexes of the songs by topic and first line. No mention of a creed. The Baptist Faith and Message, a foundational statement of faith outlining the core doctrines of the Southern Baptist faith, must be its own separate document. In an ecumenical gesture, I printed out a copy of the Apostles' Creed. If you turn to the inside back cover of my beloved *Baptist Hymnal*, it now contains the creed.

I'm familiar with a number of churches beyond my Baptist roots these days. Every year I visit other churches. Nothing makes me feel more at home than recognizing what we're doing. I still recall the first time I attended Catholic Mass with my high school friend and her family. Other than how loudly (and sometimes off-key) her dad sang, there's one other thing I distinctly remember. At some point we prayed the Lord's Prayer. It was the only part I could participate in because, although I've never attended a church where we prayed it every week, I had memorized it in Bible drills. I wasn't Catholic but this prayer connected me to them. Now, when I am a guest, the Apostles' Creed can be another thing we have in common. Many creedal churches recite the Nicene Creed when celebrating the Eucharist and the Apostles' Creed as part of the baptismal liturgy, so I guess I should get to work committing the Nicene Creed to memory too. Let me grab a notebook and a pen.

There's another reason I stubbornly cling to the creeds. To explain this well, I'd like to say a bit more about my dad. He's such a huge part of my faith story.

As a refresher, here's some background information on Dad. He was unchurched and in the words of Bible teacher Beth Moore, when talking about the prodigal son, he did some "wild living." In my finite understanding of God and the salvation he offers, I don't know if my dad was saved. I struggled with this for some time, but ultimately it taught me to place things I don't understand in God's capable hands. I loved my dad, although he was not always easy to love. In my childhood, he would disappear for a few days at a time on drinking binges. Every now and then, he came home drunk, and I couldn't tell you which one of these scenarios I preferred. There were key events in my life (i.e., baptism, school plays, graduations) he did not attend. Either he couldn't or he wouldn't. I've spent a lot of time and words and thoughts figuring out what it meant for me to love my earthly father and my heavenly father, with several key differences. Praise God he's shown me that in any number of ways, big and small, our earthly daddies of course won't measure up to God.

When Dad passed away, I grieved. With every birthday and anniversary, and elsewhere in between, I still do. Even before I consciously remember certain dates, my body seems to react to missing him, by crying for no apparent reason or an ache in my heart. The whole day feels off somehow, and I'll suddenly remember why. Now I know to turn on my George Jones playlist or find old pictures. Memory Lane is open, and although it's not free of potholes, it's a picturesque gravel road overall.

I love my dad. Full stop. However, as it turned out, I needed help in learning how to love him in a healthy way. In my twenties, I saw a therapist for a brief time. Initially, my purpose in going was for another reason altogether. Every session, though, we ended up talking about my relationship with my dad. Finally, it made sense. In relationships with men, I have to be careful. Not only in the dating ones of my twenties, but in work, friendships, and so forth. My father was absent at times and I internalized that to mean I hadn't earned his approval. I have a deep need to earn the approval of authority figures in my life, especially men. Realizing this wound opened my eyes to the tendency. When I interact in work situations, as an example, I'm aware I might need a person's approval more than I should. It can rob me of sharing my opinions, expressing my feelings, or standing in opposition. Most of the time, I handle these situations much better simply because I'm aware of how my past influences my behavior.

Our past church life influences our behavior too. Like I did with my dad, we must learn how to deal with our relationship with church in a healthy way. That might even take help from a professional, like a spiritual director or therapist. I know a lot about the Bible and church. However, as it turns out, I didn't always exercise my beliefs in a healthy, community-focused way. I've made my share of Catholic jokes. I had convinced myself those who prayed the same formal prayers every single Sunday must be saying them mechanically. This was a terrible misunderstanding of the word, rote. I've made assumption after assumption, and the more I open my mind and my heart and my ears, the assumptions prove false. Godly people do the very things I have judged and deepen their faith as a result. I'm aware of it now. There's no going back. When my Southern-Baptist-roots self looks at the creeds, whose words Southern Baptists do believe but choose not to affirm, I cannot accept being noncreedal. I embrace the creeds because my brothers and sisters in Christ do. They did for thousands of years before I came along and they will into all eternity. Why would I abandon them, the belief statements of the body of Christ, in this way? I've become hyperaware of the practices that we let divide us, and when these things do not pit me against God, I'm embracing them. The practice may not be for me, or simply not for me right now, but that's all right. At least I've learned from another Christian. This is my ongoing, active response to Paul's reminder, "There is one body and one Spirit" (Ephesians 4:4).

CHAPTER 30

Make Disciples

There are two ways, one of life and ono of death, and there
is a great difference between the two ways.

—The Didache

When we find ourselves on shaky ground, we often look back into our
past, longing for those things that have given us a firm foundation. By remembering what we know to be true, and who
we can turn to for help, because we have before, we can face our
current challenges with greater confidence. The development of
catechism questions and answers was meant to help with spiritual
formation and discipleship of children and converts to Christianity. By emphasizing memorization, responses would then be available throughout one's life, whenever people needed to be reminded
of what they believed. What has captured me about the teaching
of catechism (a term unfamiliar to me as a young believer) is the
way these memorized words get into the heart of a Christ-follower.
When life seems to be falling apart, our minds are going to turn to
something. The lessons and affirmations of the catechisms, scripture itself, formal prayers, hymns, any number of spiritual truths,
support us during those times and we can stand firm against the
trials, because they point us again to Jesus.

The oldest catechism comes from the church fathers, written
between 65 and 80 CE, and is called the Didache (or "The Teaching of the Apostles"). Although this text was lost for centuries, a
Greek copy, dated 1056, was found in 1873 and published in 1883.

Fragments with various translations have been unearthed in other geographical locales. This document of ritual instruction highlights about twenty sayings of Jesus Christ and is among the first known instructions for celebrating baptism and the Eucharist.

Like the creeds, the catechisms remind us of our Christian heritage. What we believe, and all those who have believed before us, and those who will believe after we've departed this earth. Feel the strength in the body of Christ. I've read through a variety of catechisms and what stands out to me is how much we agree on across all the questions and answers. Further, the amount of scripture used to prepare these questions and answers is inspiring.

Another reason I'm interested in considering these various historic catechisms coming out of the European Reformation period is they point to a very shaky time, the wild, wild west of Church history. As whole churches split apart, families were divided, and persecution ensued, believers needed solid footing. They believed in Jesus, but why couldn't they get along? Catechism teaching pointed believers back to scripture, helping them reestablish fundamental truths in their lives. They are teaching tools that illustrate some key points in historical context.

Learning doctrine and the foundations of faith through a catechistic process is still in use today. Many churches don't offer it in quite the same structured way of years past, but the process of leading converts and young people through a series of classes is still there. As a friend put it when he wrote to me on the topic, "If when I say the word 'catechism' you think of a book or a class, and not an all-encompassing process of enculturation, education, and reorganization of life that conforms the mind-body-spirit to the life of the Church, there's a problem." Really, what we're going for is a mere part of the introduction to a believer's lifestyle. This looks different in our various traditions, but the process is there. I've discovered another thing of beauty that has happened among these historic words. They've crept into our souls as well. Words meant to teach us have become sources of deep comfort and connectivity.

Let's look at three historic questions and answers to give you an idea of what catechisms have to offer. Even among those who remember sitting in catechism class as drudgery, these words often grow in emotional significance over time.

Anglican Middle Catechism

written in 1572 by Rev. Alexander Nowell, the dean of St. Paul's Cathedral in London.

Q: Tell me, my Child, of what Religion thou art?

A: Of the same Religion which our Saviour taught, whereof I am called and do trust that indeed I am a Christian.

Westminster Short Catechism

Q1: What is the chief end of man?

A1: Man's chief end is to glorify God, and to enjoy him for ever.

Here are the scripture references: Psalm 73:25–28; Romans 11:36; 1 Corinthians 10:31.

Heidelberg Catechism

Q1: What is your only comfort in life and death?

A1: That I am not my own, but belong with body and soul, both in life and in death, to my faithful Saviour Jesus Christ. He has fully paid for all my sins with his precious blood, and has set me free from all the power of the devil. He also preserves me in such a way that without the will of my heavenly Father not a hair can fall from my head; indeed, all things must work together for my salvation. Therefore, by his Holy Spirit he also assures me of eternal life and makes me heartily willing and ready from now on to live for him.

Here are the scripture references: Matthew 10:29–31; Luke 21:16–18; John 6:39–40; 8:34–36; 10:27–30; Romans 8:14–16, 8:28; 14:7–9; 1 Corinthians 3:23; 6:19–20; 2 Corinthians 1:21–22; 5:5; Ephesians 1:13–14; 2 Thessalonians 3:3; Titus 2:14; Hebrews 2:14–15; 1 Peter 1:5, 18–19; 1 John 1:7; 2:2; 3:8.

I asked a friend in the Presbyterian tradition to share about her interactions with the Westminster Catechism, specifically question and answer one. April, who copastors a congregation and is an author, answered me with the following:

I'm a relatively new person to the Presbyterian Church, but the Westminster Shorter Catechism Q/A1 would've been just what I needed when I was trying to figure out what I would be "when I grow up," or for those seasons of doubt and questioning when life feels so confusing. Exclusive language aside, this question and answer reminds me that no matter what season of life I'm in, no matter how certain or tumultuous, my life calling is the same. To glorify God and delight in the goodness of God all the days of my life. How seemingly simple, but also how comforting.

When I told my pastor about this book idea, we discussed the various things Christians can rely on during shaky times. Heidelberg Catechism question and answer one came up. He got a faraway look in his eyes and said, "This is probably going to be a side of me you've never seen." He told me about times when he has put his head quite close to another person's on a pillow while they were sick in the hospital or at home. They're often from an older generation, and he knows they'll find comfort in these particular words. Reaching his arm up, arcing as if cupping an individual's head in the crook of his arm, he leans in close and whispers softly, "What is your only comfort in life and in death?"

These words have been touched by the spirit of the living God. For some of our brothers and sisters, they have moved beyond head knowledge into the depths of their very heart. It reminds me of a hymn we used to sing, "If you would join the glad songs of the blest, Let Jesus come into your heart."

In the midst of writing this chapter, I came across a Heidelberg Catechism story in a rather unusual place. I like a good historical fiction read because I can combine learning with great storytelling. I was reading Lynn Austin's *Chasing Shadows*, which is about a family in the Netherlands who found themselves unable to remain neutral as the Nazis moved into their country in World War II. One ill-fated afternoon the daughter is returning to the place where she is staying and is captured by Nazi soldiers. During the ensuing interrogation, she's understandably scared out of her mind. Austin writes: "Terror flooded through her. Then, unbidden, the words Ans had been made to memorize in catechism class swirled through her mind, *'I am not my own, but I belong body and soul, in life and in death, to my faithful Savior, Jesus Christ.'"* She experienced a peace and calm, even in the most dire of circumstances.

Catechisms help us get to know one another. People from older generations can have a particular affinity for the questions and answers they learned as children. Others might look for doctrinal points they disagree with, and perhaps there's a time and place for that. I hope you also see the universal truths these documents can offer us. When our posture is one of honest curiosity, and we take delight in learning from one another, we better see we have more in common than we thought we did, and discover the shared ground beneath our feet may be more solid than we realized.

CHAPTER 31

Abiding as Spiritual Practice

I have said these things to you so that my joy may be in
you, and that your joy may be complete.

—John 15:11

As we near the end of this book, I hope you've found some new ways
to connect with Jesus and are more convinced than ever that
we need one another to live into the fullness of Christ. Most of
all, I hope you can stand a little stronger, even if the ground below
you is shaking. When the bottom drops out, God is still there, helping us pick up the pieces, and doing a work in us, through whatever
hard things we've endured.

In Jesus's last few hours on earth, he shared a final meal with
his closest companions. The gospel of John provides the largest
portion of text on what we know as the Last Supper. When reading
John chapters thirteen through seventeen, I often ask myself: If I
knew this was my last meal with loved ones, what would I most
want to share?

Being ecumenically minded, I'm wild, of course, about the
closing prayer where Jesus prayed we would be one. "I ask not
only on behalf of these, but also on behalf of those who will
believe in me through their word, that they may all be one. As
you, Father, are in me and I am in you, may they also be in us, so
that the world may believe that you have sent me" (John 17:20–
21). When I realize the unity, even among our differences, Jesus
wanted us to have, my heart breaks. We don't have this and many
of us aren't fostering a faith community that promotes it. The

184

church should stand as a beacon of solidarity, but instead we're often part of the problem.

I wish we'd focus more on how we can work together to make this happen as individuals and as part of a community of faith. What is the spirit's role in carrying this out? Does God really expect us to find unity in these polarizing times? How could this help Christians stand on solid ground when everything around us seems shaky? These are all good questions to consider.

Before this prayer for unity, Jesus refers to himself as the vine in the fifteenth chapter of John. "Abide in me as I abide in you. Just as the branch cannot bear fruit by itself unless it abides in the vine, neither can you unless you abide in me. I am the vine, you are the branches. Those who abide in me and I in them bear much fruit, because apart from me you can do nothing" (John 15:4–5). A few verses later, he adds, "My Father is glorified by this, that you bear much fruit and become my disciples" (John 15:8). Then, later he tells us the fruit that comes from abiding in him will last (John 15:16).

Abide in him as a disciple and bear fruit. What an invitation. I've messed this up more times over the years than I can count, but Jesus doesn't say to get your act together and then come to him. He doesn't ask us to work harder. He doesn't say he's keeping score.

The word for "abide" in this chapter is the Greek word *meno*, a primary verb. Think back to English class. What is a verb? The action word in a sentence. Jesus uses this action word thirteen times in this chapter. I'm thinking he's saying something pretty important. Enough so that he's given us countless ways to abide in him—spiritual practices. Here's the invitation: to abide, to remain in him. In his final words, he didn't get specific about doctrinal stances, or clear up theological debates. If I may paraphrase, he said stick with me, and I will stick with you.

I did a quick search online and found other English words that are synonyms for *meno*. Read them slowly and add "in Jesus" after each word. This is what he wants for us. To stay [in Jesus], continue, dwell, endure, be present, remain, stand, sojourn, to be held, kept, continually.

Finally, tarry. We never have to rush our time with Jesus. If the intentional time we've set apart is interrupted, he's there waiting when we return. It's true as well that he's always with us. How do we abide? You know by now. In silence, in prayer, in reading scripture, in getting to know our brothers and sisters in Christ, in the sacraments, in liturgy, in the creeds and catechisms. Anything that helps us focus on Jesus, finding ourselves following in his firm footsteps.

Abide in Jesus and his great love. Become his disciples and bear much fruit. We don't even have to worry about producing spiritual fruit—it's a supernatural by-product of abiding in Jesus. Lasting fruit, such as unity in the body of Christ, celebrates our diversity. Complete joy. A life of steadfastness we cannot find in quick fixes. A living hope that others will want you to explain (1 Peter 3:15). And in doing this, God is glorified (John 15:8). Unbelievable.

Epilogue

was telling a pastor friend, Matt, about being a big fan of a sanctuary, holy spaces: "About a month into the pandemic, I was like, I have a key to my church. If I could sneak in at night, and just sit in the sanctuary, that would do my soul so much good."

"What stopped you from going in that night," he asked, "using the key that you had? Have you reflected on that and wondered why?"

I didn't have a good answer for him. During quarantine, when the whole world went shaky, sitting in my church sanctuary would have helped. However, I'm enough of a rule follower to adhere to the policies put in place to keep our building clean, so when we could gather again, we would do so safely. I wasn't about to contaminate that sacred space with my germs. When we did finally go back to in-person worship, it felt wonderful to sit in that sanctuary again, in the midst of the people of God.

In the early stages of writing this book, I started out with a list of spiritual practices that an individual could use. I realized pretty quickly any discipline that helps you mature as a person of faith, also helps the body of believers. We're always living in community, under the headship of Christ.

Then I looked at the gifts of the church and recognized they too have great significance in an individual's life, but are meant to be shared. When we come together and learn from one another, we better experience the abundant life Christ promised his followers. And in the land of abundant living, tethered to Jesus and one another, we become unshakable. "Do not be conformed to this world, but be transformed by the renewing of your minds, so that you may discern what is the will of God—what is good and acceptable and perfect" (Romans 12:2). Discipleship—we do it together. We still sin, but know to ask God to cleanse us and purify our hearts (James 4:8). There's still shaky ground, but we know with God as our rock and salvation, we will not be shaken (Psalm 62:6). Not permanently.

There's something natural and inborn in us that longs for the sacred things of God. That's meant to come together with others. We might sing hymns or pray the Lord's Prayer or recite a creed or answer catechism questions or sit in silence or read a psalm or offer a confession or receive a blessing. All of this is good, but nothing beats communing at the table, hearing those sacred words; take, eat—this is my body broken for you.

Does this mean there's never a good reason to step away from the church for a time? We can all think of legitimate times a person or family might need to do this. What's important to remember, even during those times when we aren't part of a local body of believers, we're still a vital part of the body of Christ. We cannot separate.

If you're not attending a church at the moment, if you're in the midst of redefining church in your life, when you're ready to return, I'll save you a seat. You can always sit with me. In every congregation, in every city, in every state, in every country around the world, may God raise up deeply welcoming people.

When things are going well, it's hard to know what might end up being most precious to us when we lack. In our personal lives, when things start to unravel, we need the common threads of faith. It is through these practices that God draws near. They are timeless. They are precious. I'll leave you with this: "Therefore, my beloved, be steadfast, immovable, always excelling in the work of the Lord, because you know that in the Lord your labor is not in vain" (1 Corinthians 15:58). But also, true to the cry of my own spiritual heartbeat, the lyrics from a beloved hymn, "The Old Rugged Cross":

> So I'll cherish the old rugged cross,
> Till my trophies at last I lay down;
> I will cling to the old rugged cross,
> And exchange it some day for a crown.

Acknowledgments

These acknowledgments encompass much more than a simple thanks to those who helped in the writing of this particular book. The people I mention here walk with me on this faith journey. They play different roles, but we'll continue on together long after readers set this book down.

To Ryan, the ways we "talk" about faith by living it every day have taught me that it's about so much more than words. To Allie, you show up on so many pages of this book, and that's because I want more than anything to show you Jesus Christ, and his body, the Church, in all their glory.

To my agent, Jim, you understood my work from the very first e-mail I sent you, and never waver in your support. Thank you. To my editor, Nancy, I can't wait to meet in person someday. Every correct high church term in this book comes from your wealth of knowledge. To my editorial and marketing partners at Church Publishing, you make the book better. Period.

To the women of North Point, we're sharing more of our stories here. Let's keep at it.

To the Twitter Church community, don't ever let anyone tell you nothing good comes from social media. I'm a fool for trying to list those who have influenced me, because I'll leave people out, but I'm going to give it a try. Thank you for listening to me think out loud, and for answering all my questions. You satisfy my endless curiosity in a deeply meaningful way. Let's all meet up for dinner: Aarik, Aaron, Adam, Aida, Alex, Angela, Anna-Kate, Andrew, Anya, April, Art, Barbara, Becky, Ben, Bill, Brent, Bryn, Buz, Cara, Caroline, Catherine, Charles, Chuck, Connie, Courtney, Dallas, Damon, Dana, Daniel, Daryl, David, Dawn, Dottie, Douglas,

Drew, Ed, Edwin, Eliza, Emily, Eric, Erik, Erma, Frank, Gary, Gena, Gene, Geoffrey, Gerald, Ginny, Gordon, Greg, Gretchen, Ian, James, Janean, Janson, Jason, Jeanie, Jeffrey, Jenn, Jenni, Jeremy, Jill, Jim, Joan, Jody, Jon, Jonathan, Jonny, Joseph, Josh, Josiah, Joy, Julia, Julian, Kara, Karen, Kathy, Kate, Katie, Keith, Kelly, Kerry, Kevin, Kristy, Kristopher, Lana, Laura, Laurie, Lee, Leo, Lisa, Lore, Malinda, Marcus, Margaret, Marina, Mark, Matt, Megan, Meir, Michael, Monica, Nicole, Noel, Pam, Pat, Phil, Phoebe, Rachel, Randy, Robert, Ron, Ruth, Ryan, Sam, Sarah, Scott, Shane, Shaneen, Shemiah, Steve, Sujit, Summer, Tanya, Terry, Timothy, Tina, Tom, Trish, Wendy, Yonadav.

Appendix of Practices

The following is a list of the *grounding words* used to name each section of this book. Also, a particular spiritual practice I have found especially meaningful that speaks to each word, and recommended books that helped me understand how to fit this discipline into my ongoing rhythm.

Solid Ground (Silence)

I've taken to calling it the *ministry of presence*. We have a teenage daughter, and there are times I sense she needs me to just sit with her. No questions, no advice, until she's ready. Seated side by side, a visible reminder that she is not alone.

I've also implemented this ministry style with those who are suffering mentally or physically. No words, unless they want to talk. Silence has a healing power of its own, and when we sit with one another, we'll actually find ourselves standing together on solid ground.

Books

Acedia & Me: A Marriage, Monks, and a Writer's Life by Kathleen
  Norris
Everything Happens for a Reason: And Other Lies I've Loved by Kate
  Bowler

Stability (Prayer)

A few years back, I began reading a formal prayer book, such as the Book of Common Prayer, first thing in the morning. I'm sure I don't use it properly, but I've found particular prayers and written statements that I offer up as meaningful worship to God, before my mind has formed a single prayer of its own. They are my spiritual wake-up call. There's stability in relying on the prayers of others.

I rotate through prayer books and books of poetry in my mornings. I'm not sure when I began using poetry in these earliest moments of the day, but I recognize they give my spirit a first morsel of literary food. I'm not quite ready for a scriptural workout yet, but the poems serve as warm-up exercises, my spiritual stretches.

Books

Pray Like a Gourmet: Creative Ways to Feed Your Soul by David Brazzeal
The Divine Hours: Pocket Edition by Phyllis Tickle

Anchored (Bible Reading)

Learning to read the Bible with fluidity has been perhaps the biggest area of growth for me. When I pick up God's word, am I studying it, reading it like a novel, or praying it? It's become natural for me to ebb and flow, in and out, of all these reading styles.

This really comes to life for me when I read passages out loud. Vocalizing what I'm reading calls to mind, this is the way people would have interacted with scripture for thousands of years, having it read to them. Reading the Bible out loud brings me fresh insight, as certain words seem especially significant, and reading with inflection gives me a better idea of the emotions presented in the passage. Scripture is our steadfast anchor in a shaky world.

Books

Eat This Book: A Conversation in the Art of Spiritual Reading by Eugene Peterson
Reading the Bible with Rabbi Jesus: How a Jewish Perspective Can Transform Your Understanding by Lois Tverberg

Foundation (Church History)

History often takes on more meaning as we get older. Perhaps it's because we actually begin to have some history of our own as we age. In the past five years, I've taken a deep dive into church history. Solomon was right, there's nothing new under the sun (Ecclesiastes 1:9). What that really means is we stand on a firm foundation. Yes, there are lessons to learn from the past, but two things about church history have emerged as even more important than what the past has to teach us.

First, we're part of something timeless. I've been a Protestant, right here in Midwest USA, my entire life. Our Judeo-Christian heritage goes back to the beginning, and I've stepped into it. What an honor to accept that invitation. For me, the American evangelical world has become entirely too small. Second, we've received the gift of wisdom from the past. Not only can we mine the Bible for endless treasure, we can learn from every culture, time, and place through the written word and church tradition.

Books

Christian History Made Easy by Paul Timothy Jones
The Church History ABCs [with the children] by Stephen J. Nichols and Ned Bustard
The Ecumenism of Beauty compiled by Timothy Verdon

Assurance (Gifts of the Church)

As my Christianity expanded, I had this sense I'd missed out on so many of the practices the larger Church offers believers. Not only practices, but fellowship with one another. I rarely call communion the Lord's Supper anymore. Eucharist feels too formal for my country girl upbringing. But *communion*, I participate in that whenever two or three gather together in his name. Blessed assurance, Jesus is mine (ours). The Orthodox offer me antidoron, the blessed but not consecrated, bread. Catholics offer me a priestly blessing, with a reverent nod to Numbers 6:24–26. Many of your own churches invite me to the communion table with you. I'll never get over the bread and the wine. Here we are together, waiting for the moment Jesus promised us: "I tell you, I will never again drink of this fruit of the vine until that day when I drink it new with you in my Father's kingdom" (Matthew 26:29).

Books

Out of the House of Bread: Satisfying Your Hunger for God with the Spiritual Disciplines by Preston Yancey
Mudhouse Sabbath: An Invitation to a Life of Spiritual Discipline by Lauren Winner

References

These are the references I mentioned (in order of appearance)—you may appreciate them as well.

Prologue: Shaky Ground

While You Were Sleeping. Directed by Jon Turteltaub, performances by Sandra Bullock and Bill Pullman. Hollywood Pictures in association with Caravan Pictures, 1998.

Chapter Two

Aaron Niequist, *The Eternal Current: How a Practice-Based Faith Can Save Us* (New York: WaterBrook, 2018), 51.

Chapter Three

Rich Villodas, *The Deeply Formed Life: Five Transformative Values to Root Us in the Way of Jesus* (Colorado Springs, CO: WaterBrook, 2020), xxviii.

Chapter Four

J. Brent Bill, *Holy Silence: The Gift of Quaker Spirituality* (Grand Rapids, MI: Eerdmans, 2016), 109, 107.

Chapter Six

Shūsaku Endō, *Silence: A Novel*, trans. William Johnston (New York: Picador Modern Classics; trans. ed., 2016), 106.

Lisa Colón DeLay, *The Wild Land Within: Cultivating Wholeness through Spiritual Practice* (Minneapolis: Broadleaf Books, 2021), 100.

Chapter Eight

Tish Harrison Warren, *Prayer in the Night: For Those Who Work or Watch or Weep* (Downers Grove, IL: InterVarsity Press, 2021), 7.

Chapter Nine

Kate Bowler, *Everything Happens for a Reason: And Other Lies I've Loved* (New York: Random House, 2018), 121.

"Not All Those Who Wander Are Lost." YouTube, uploaded by Kevin Barhydt, July 28, 2021, *www.youtube.com/watch?v=1Q7x8wIhSdk&t=1s.*

Chapter Ten

W. David O. Taylor, *Open and Unafraid: The Psalms as a Guide to Life* (Nashville: Thomas Nelson Books, 2020), 15.

Kathleen Norris, *The Cloister Walk* (New York: Riverhead, 1996), 93.

Chapter Thirteen

Esau McCauley, *Reading While Black: African American Biblical Interpretation as an Exercise in Hope* (Downers Grove, IL: InterVarsity Press Academic, 2020), 20–21.

Rebbetzin Dena Weinberg, "Twenty Favorite Jewish Quotes," *aish*, accessed November 16, 2021, *www.aish.com/sp/ph/20-Favorite-Jewish-Quotes. html.*

Chapter Fourteen

Hilary Yancey, *Forgiving God: A Story of Faith* (New York: FaithWords, 2018), 21.

Chapter Sixteen

Eugene Peterson, *Eat This Book: A Conversation in the Art of Spiritual Reading* (Grand Rapids, MI: Eerdmans, 2006), 50.

"St. Patrick's Breastplate: A Shield for Divine Protection," *Our Catholic Prayers*, accessed December 12, 2021, *www.ourcatholicprayers.com/ st-patricks-breastplate.html.*

Chapter Seventeen

Enzira Sebhat, *Harp of Glory: An Alphabetical Hymn of Praise for the Ever-Blessed Virgin Mary from the Ethiopian Orthodox Church* (Yonkers, NY: St. Vladimir's Seminary Press, 2010), 9–10, 35–36.

Martin Luther. "Martin Luther (founder of the reformed), speaks on Mary," *Catholic Bridge*, accessed December 12, 2021, *www.catholic-bridge.com/catholic/martin-luther-on-mary.php*.

St. Anthony the Great, "Sayings of St Anthony the Great," *Orthodox Chattanooga*, accessed December 1, 2021, *www.orthodoxchattanooga.com/ news/2021/1/18/sayings-of-st-anthony-the-great*.

Chapter Nineteen

Shawn Smucker, *Once We Were Strangers: What Friendship with a Syrian Refugee Taught Me about Loving My Neighbor* (Grand Rapids, MI: Revell, 2018), 173.

Chapter Twenty

Hildegard of Bingen, "Hildegard of Bingen Quotes," *Healthy Hildegard*, accessed December 1, 2021, *www.healthyhildegard.com/hildegard-bingen-quotes*.

Cheryl Anne Tuggle, *Lights on the Mountain: A Novel* (Brewster, MA: Paraclete Press, 2019), 83, 84.

Chapter Twenty-Five

Barbara Brown Taylor, *Always a Guest: Speaking of Faith Far from Home* (Louisville, KY: Westminster John Knox Press, 2020), x.

Chapter Twenty-Six

Margaret Feinberg, *Taste and See: Discovering God among Butchers, Bakers, & Fresh Food Makers* (Grand Rapids, MI: Zondervan, 2019), 89–90.

Chapter Twenty-Seven

Rachel Marie Stone, *Birthing Hope: Giving Fear to the Light* (Downers Grove, IL: InterVarsity Press, 2018), 86.

Chapter Twenty-Eight

Anne Brontë, "The Doubter's Prayer," in *Poems by Currer, Ellis, and Acton Bell* (Philadelphia: Lea and Blanchard, 1848), 86.

Chapter Twenty-Nine

"The Apostles' Creed," *bcponline*, accessed October 15, 2021, *https://bcp online.org/DailyOffice/mp2.html*.

Paul Senz, "The How and the Why of the Nicene Creed," *Catholic Answers*, February 1, 2021, *https://www.catholic.com/magazine/print-edition/ the-how-and-why-of-the-nicene-creed*.

"The Nicene Creed," *bcponline*, accessed October 15, 2021, *www.bcp online.org/General/nicene_creed.html*.

Luke Timothy Johnson, *The Creed: What Christians Believe and Why It Matters* (New York: Image, 2004), 40–41.

Chapter Thirty

Alexander Nowell, "Middle Catechism or the Institution of Christian Religion," *anglican.net*, accessed October 17, 2021, *https://www.angli-can.net/works/alexander-nowell-middle-catechism-or-the-institu-tion-of-christian-religion-1572/*.

"Shorter Catechism: Text and Scripture Proofs," *The Westminster's Standard*, accessed October 17, 2021, *https://thewestminsterstandard. org/westminster-shorter-catechism/*.

"Heidelberg Catechism," *Christian Reformed Church of North America*, accessed October 17, 2021, *https://www.crcna.org/sites/default/files/ HeidelbergCatechism.pdf*.

Lynn Austin, *Chasing Shadows* (Carol Stream, IL: Tyndale House Publishers, 2021), 323.

About the Author

Traci Rhoades is a writer, Bible teacher, and follower of Jesus who cares deeply about church unity, church history, and everyone reading God's word. She lives in the Grand Rapids, Michigan, area with her family. She is the author of the award-winning book, *Not All Who Wander (Spiritually) Are Lost.* Connect with her online at tracesoffaith.com or @tracesoffaith on Twitter.